Chanticleer

A Memoir of Light and Love

by Marney Jane Blair

Printed in the United States of America

First Printing, 2014

ISBN 9781633183407

Bookpatch Publishing

www.thebookpatch.com

To my wife Lisa,

my farming partner.

Acknowledgments

I would like to thank Susan Bono, editor and teacher extraordinaire, for generously helping me shape my writing into a book.

I thank Linda Jane for editing my wild drafts.

A big hug to my sister in law, Gigia Kolough for formatting.

Thanks also to Elizabeth Lane and Carin Fortin for the book cover design.

Maya Koshla

My heart extends to Rachel Carson, Sue Hubbel and Wendell Berry for the beauty in their work.

Thank you Dad and Bill.

Finally a big thanks to The Farm and all the wondrous life she holds.

CHAPTER 1

The soothing rose light caresses the inside of my sleeping eyelids. Slowly, as the energy of a new day soaks into my dream life, I move into an awakened state. I open my eyes gently and see the busy, buzzing insect air outside my bedroom window. As I watch the gliding activity, my ears pick up the rooster's call at the far end of the farm. Another glorious day on the farm is about to begin.

I walk into the kitchen to make coffee on the stove top. The aroma fills the sleepy kitchen air. While I sip I look outside the large windows and try to feel the day. This simple, momentary reflection helps guide me as I make decisions about all the animals and plants on the farm today. I chuckle to myself. Every day for twelve years, or over four thousand times, I have engaged in this helpful ritual.

I enjoy the last sip and walk toward the front door. A swirl of seductive spring air moves across my face as I walk up the short path to the milking barn. Lisa, my partner, moves her pitch fork in fluid, confident arcs as she cleans out the milking area. The earthy weight of the cow pie plopping into the wheelbarrow makes a satisfying, grounding sound. It counters the caffeine buzz.

"Wow, another beautiful morning in paradise!" I shout to Lisa as I walk up to the open pole barn.

"Isn't it amazing? " she says, with an air of excitement. "I'll finish cleaning up here. Do you wanna go and get the cows?"

"Yes, it's light enough. I can see," I say, as I walk away from the barn and on a path through a grove of live oak toward the cow's night yard.

The farm is located in the Sierra foothills of northern California. The land undulates among the valley oak groves. A stream divides the pastureland from the woodlands. The hillside is populated by gray pine, ponderosa pine, black oak, blue oak, valley oaks, alders and manzanita. The pasture flatlands are home to fescue, clover, birdsfoot trefoil and annual rye.

The farm holds seven cows in her care. There are three milking Jersey cows, three Scottish Highland-Milking Devon crosses, and one Highland bull. When watch them they seem to hold the pasture in place, an ancient marriage between plant and animal. When they lie down to ruminate, their large bodies appear to expand and fill the space with elegance. They have their eyes half closed. Many times a day they go through the exercise of regurgitating the cud and rolling it around in their mouths. The green wad slowly swirls among the molars, releasing the beautiful, vibrant juice. Each chew is a deep meditation. The digestive vapors, deep within the rumen, move up into the head and tumble out of their nostrils onto the pasture as they masticate the next wad of grass.

The cows hold the digestive rhythm of the farm. This important beat sets the productive pace of this farm. All of the other animals, including the farmers, are glad to move to this beat because we have other roles on the farm. They have earned our respect. Above all domesticated animals, the bovine provides a grounded, steady metabolic pace.

The rooster Hank sounds a muffled crow from inside the coop. He knows to be patient until the morning's milking is done. Only after the cows have been lead back to pasture and the milking pails cleaned will he be set free to stand tall in the oak grove and watch over the farm. All day long Hank will stand at attention, listening and looking for unwanted intruders. He'll watch proudly over his hens, occasionally signaling with a coo and scratching feet that he has found some good food. He'll wait for the cows to return to the pasture, for this is when he and his hens receive their glorious milk, curd or whey. He knows his role on the farm and rightfully carries it through.

The pigs sleep in. They hear the cow's feet vibrate the red clay soil as they move past their den. They hear the rooster sound off as he walks into the misty morning air. The smart pigs may stir, but they know the food is coming so why rise sooner than that. When the slop of grains and milk arrives, their noses are the first to animate their heavy, dense bodies. As the slop is poured into the trough, they are overcome with joy. They bump each other, bump the farmer, bump the tree, and stand in the trough to be with their food.

Now that the animals are settled for the morning, Lisa and I can tend to the needs of the other life forms we hold near our hearts--the plants. The plants are of the domesticated type and have been human companions for thousands of years.

Lisa and I decided eleven years ago that we would grow food crops that were seeds, rather than vegetables. Seeds that people eat are known as grains, edible seeds like sunflower or beans. Like the animals, each plant has a personality on the farm. The majestic corn towers above, reaching for the fire and holding it in her golden seed, while the bean is happy to stay low to the ground, breathing in the moist, humid earth. Later in the season the bean will produce a dense, hard and colorful seed.

As I walk about on this precious piece of land, a gift of nature, I walk tall, knowing my job and my role. I am the conductor. As a human I am bestowed the ability to perceive beyond myself and thus can tend to the needs of every animal, plant, and mineral that lives within these 20 acres. I take on this huge responsibility knowing that it is a huge opportunity to live up to my given gift on this planet.

I walk strong and proud while holding Lisa's hand, knowing that our love for each other has ignited every creative project here. I know this is home. We are here, now.

The role of the farmer is to support life, but death and disease are part of life, an inevitable part of life. Every living being has a dramatic story.

Sophie is a Jersey cow. She picked us to be her caretaker. We were sitting among the rocks at our friends' 2,000 acre ranch looking at the various heifer calves. Sophie kept walking up to us. All of the young girls were range cattle, wild and wary of humans. These dairy cows were like deer and would shy away from any movement we made. Sophie was different. She was curious and trusting of humans. While we sat among the cows on a rock outcrop, she kept moving closer to us. Lisa offered her hand as the curious heifer walked right up to us. We both got a closer look at her.

She was not a prize heifer. The young cow had healed wounds on her hide, probably from entanglements in the brush. The wounds left black scars that bore no hair. She was a bit too curious and clumsy. While she sniffed Lisa's hand, I looked at her face. She had a pirate patch over her right eye. It was made of burlap and had been attached to her face with some strange adhesive. The rancher has placed it there. He guessed that perhaps she got a sticker in her eye. The eyeball was saved, but her vision in that eye was not.

Without hesitation Lisa and I decided on Sophie.

That was three years ago.

A year later, in the spring of 2004 Sophie was pregnant with her second calf. In great anticipation, we both felt that she was going to deliver a girl. The last seven calves born to our cows were bull calves. A bull calf isn't nearly as useful as a heifer. A female cow can give you milk and sire a young. We needed a heifer to expand our dairy herd.

My deceased mother's presence was in the air around the farm that spring. This was our seventh year farming. Out of love and respect, I decided to name the calf Beverly, my mother's name, if it was a girl.

Sophie was oozing clear mucous fluids. Her delivery was only a matter of days, perhaps hours. Her udder was engorged with milk. It was so full that she couldn't walk properly. This sweet bovine had to swing her leg around inside her hip bone. Mother Nature, in her grand design, has created such indescribable beauty, but also such unmentionable pain and suffering. This cow was ready to pop. Her udder was developing edema. I gently placed my hand on her bag, and the imprint of my middle finder stayed.

We brought her into the barn.

The day turned into night and still she had not moved into labor. My brain swelled with worry. I tossed and turned and felt very sad and twisted inside. Finally, at 3am, I surrendered to my exhaustion.

I woke just before sunrise. I could feel that it wasn't a regular day. It felt crooked and craggy. The hair on the back of my head was twisted into knots. Sure enough, as the sun broke the horizon, Sophie went into labor.

When Rosa and Sara had their calves, each labor had progressed without much fanfare. Sara had her second calf while we were sleeping. The next morning we were greeted by a nursing newborn. Rosa had easy births in the barn. For each one we stood aside and let the mother's body create the opening for a new being to inhabit the earth. So far seven calves had been born on this farm.

The first time I watched a birthing it was amazing and terrifying. When a calf emerges from the watery, sleepy womb it looks dead, as if from another realm and not quite fit for the terrestrial life. However, as soon as the calf's wet, slimy body touches the earth, it has arrived and begins to breathe. The mama cow earnestly awakens the calf's nervous system. She uses her gritty tongue to clean the newborn. The delicate body rocks back and forth under the persistent, sandpaper-like cleaning.

Within an hour the calf is alert and trying to find the mother's milk. The mama moos and circles the newborn. She is busy tending her young, drinking water and listening for any unusual predatory sound. Miraculously the baby always manages to find its mama and her milk.

This morning my heart was ready, despite a night of narrow, tight dreams, to welcome yet another warm-blooded mammal into our care. We closed the door of the house behind us as we walked to the barn. Sure enough, Sophie was hunched over with contractions. Lisa went to the garage to fetch a bucket of hot water.

I stood and watched over the cow. Sophie grunted and a white sack began to emerge. Even after seven calves our minds were not registering that this was unusual. Finally, I was able to digest the sight that was before my eyes. The entire embryonic sac was emerging. During normal calving the calf moves into position while in the womb and eventually breaks the tough sheath of the sac as it emerges from its mother.

But this time the calf was encased within the watery sac. The mother was pushing out the entire sack. Lisa and I froze in disbelief. Something was terribly wrong.

We began to talk in fast, tense questions. Then we jumped into action, as it was obvious we needed to help. Lisa sprinted indoors to dial our vet. I jumped into the manger and began to tear open the three membranous layers of the sac. They were warm, tough, elastic and very slippery. I eventually managed to rip the tissues and expose the calf's moist, delicate nostrils to the air. I stuck my fingers into the nostrils to remove the viscous mucous. They were so small that I had a hard time effectively cleaning the air passage. I fumbled and stumbled with urgency.

The mama cow and I were moaning together. "Come on, little one, take in that air." The anguish and anxiety were unbearable. The cow was licking her head as I tried to clear the mucous.

I jiggled the head. Still no response.

She was a beautiful, hazel-colored jersey. So delicate, with her white hooves still soft from the watery environment in which she had developed. Everything looked perfect. Her eyes were a deep brown, just like her mother's. She had long legs and velvet ears.

"Come on, sweet thing, breathe!"

But she was gone.

In the process of moving from one state of being to another, she was not able to make the transition. She was unable to rip through and come crashing into the, oh, so physical world. Instead, in her soft, damp, dreamy world she remained.

Immediately after the calf fell to the ground I was immersed in a heavy, humid, emotional world. The mama cow was moaning and desperately licking her young. How deeply I felt her sorrow as I silently watched her. Lisa joined me. We both wanted to comfort her.

"I'm driving over to Mike's. He may have a newborn we can give to Sophie," Lisa yelled and jumped over the fence and into the car. The car roared up the driveway and she was gone.

Emotionally exhausted, I sat in the wet straw next to Sophie. I could hear in her moans and callings the desperate sorrow. As one female mammal to another female mammal, I understood that this was a primal hurt, a hurt that echoed throughout our clear creek valley.

Beverly.

Yes, this was the calf we had decided to name after my mom.

Now I had a dead Beverly. Another dead Beverly.

The idea of naming the calf after my mom came to us within weeks of my decision to write this book. The coming together of the collective muse to write the book shared the same timestamp as the decision to connect this life with the essence of my mom. It seemed easy enough at the time.

Easy until I found myself burying the calf in the garden.

I was in a daze digging the hole. I had to dig a deep hole, for she was an 80-pound calf. When I finished digging the hole, I gazed at a pink rose bush. It was growing vigorously in front of the chicken coop. That felt right for this sweet little calf; the rose would be in bloom and smell good in the summer heat.

I heard the car enter the driveway and the door shut. Lisa walked toward the open garden gate. Her head was low, her eyes focused on the ground. I could tell by her body language that Mike didn't have a calf. Our eyes met, and without saying anything, we both knew that it had been a futile idea to find a calf for Sophie. But I knew that Lisa needed to try. We embraced.

We walked over to the barn, Sophie was still licking her calf. We waited. We waited for an hour, until she began to eat her alfalfa and give up on licking her calf. The calf was cold. Sophie was tired and hungry. I picked up the calf and placed it in a wheelbarrow.

"I'll bury her," I said in a tone that let Lisa know that I wanted to bury the calf alone.

As I heaved the calf into the hole I said to myself, finally I get to bury you, Mom. I wasn't shocked by this statement. It was grounding and cathartic. I sat on the damp clay soil and let the internal storm of sorrow pass.

Yes, I was burying Beverly in my own time and in my own space. I needed to touch that calf's body, feel the coldness of the dead flesh again. I was actively moving the memory of my mother to another space in my heart.

My mother had died ten years earlier.

In the hospital I had sat by her side holding her hand. Her body convulsed under unbearable pain. The emotional pain surged periodically like a high tide. She hadn't wanted to die. Her anger swelled and made her weak body twist and turn, back and forth in the metal bed. I felt my mind knot in confusion over such unearthly suffering. I glanced at my sister-in-law sitting at the edge of my mother's bed. Our eyes met and I felt connected again to the sane thread of reality.

"Mom, it's ok to let go. You need to let yourself leave in peace," I said with confidence. The time to surrender was now. Seven years of suffering had come to an end.

My mother's body was sent away to be cremated. Eventually her ashes showed up in a cardboard box. The box remained above my father's closet for a long time. No one knew what to do with it. I had no relationship to it. It was a strange thing, a small cardboard box, three quarters full of gray ashes. They were a cold gray. They did not feel like Beverly.

This calf was real for me, and I was able to place some of my emotional needs onto her precious, vulnerable body. I finally stood up from the mound near the rose and walked to the barn. Sophie was still circling the area looking for her calf. Lisa was working silently, cleaning up the blood and tissue.

Membranes that are still enlivened by blood have a wonderful light emerging from them. The sac that held the calf hung from Sophie. It had a moonlight whiteness to it. We stood there and gazed at its luminosity, stunned by its beauty and vitality. It was dotted with the most brilliant red saucers. They were shimmering with life, full of red blood and moist warmth. Each red spot was the size of a tea cup saucer and had been attached to Sophie's uterus. Their redness was in surreal contrast to the cool, white color of the sac. I kept saying in my mind, this color and light is otherworldly. It was a kind of light that you can feel when looking at stars. Not a terrestrial light but a light from far, far away.

Suddenly gravity forced the sac to the ground.

Sophie, still moaning for her loss, began to slowly slurp the giant sac into her mouth. Occasionally she was able to tear a piece off and swallow it. I watched this instinctive primal act in silence. She was taking the celestial light back into her body.

I watched and ate this universal light with my eyes.

CHAPTER 2

I hold yellow and maroon seeds. I planted their parent plants six months earlier. Now that the green bean plants have created the pods for their young, the plants will wither and die. By Halloween, all the annuals will die and leave their offspring to survive the cold winter.

I love to hold the fruits of our labors. Running my hands through the barrels of corn and sorghum seed stored in our barn, I travel back in time to the early spring. Lisa and I planted all this season's plants by hand, each seed cupped gently in our palms.

We planted three acres this year. For the corn and beans, we use a wooden stamp to make a diamond pattern in the bed. We place each seed in a divot in the moist soil, crawling next to each other on our hands and knees as we move down the row pushing the seeds into the warm bed. Our meandering conversation warms the seeds as they move from our palms to the soil. After placing each seed in the divot, we gently cover it with a mound of dirt.

Hands are the real tools of a farmer. These tools are sensitive and can serve as a conduit between the farmer's will and the object she is touching. Sorghum and sesame twirl in the fingers as they cascade into their furrows. Squash seeds need a thumb to press them into a mound. The flax, an oily seed, requires a certain fling of the finger to set it free. If she cares to, a farmer can move love for that object through her hands.

My wife's hands are strong from years of hard labor, but they're also sensitive like the artist she is. In the same day she can build a chicken coop and gently rub salve on my tired back. The skin on her right hand is scarred from burns endured as a young adult. Her hands, like her solid hips and shoulders, thick salt and pepper hair, and fearless eyes, project strength and confidence.

Lisa arrived on this land before I did. When she was a young adult, her father had taught her to target shoot on the site that our house now occupies. She knew the oak groves that fed the deer and wild turkeys. She knew the thick brush that lined the creekside. In her late thirties, she decided to make it her home. Lisa's mother, passing on her inheritance to her daughters, provided the financing for what became a two-year project to build a house. Her brother-in-law provided the design, but Lisa provided the labor. A hard job for a man, an even harder job for a woman.

When I first stepped into her home several years later, I could see the loving craftswomanship. Even though we had met just a few months earlier, I knew that we would build our dreams together. I could sense that we would be each other's muse, and that our hands would weave a magical tapestry of life.

Together we could see the beginnings of a farm.

"Look Marn, this would be a fantastic spot for the first growing area!" Lisa said, as we walked through the tall grasses and around a large outcropping of boulders. She had walked this field many times while she was building her house, and she had had her eye on it. She knew the types of plants that grew here and how the water moved during winter rain storms.

"Let's stand here and see," I replied. I listened to the wind move through the grass. We both knew that an open flat field with full sunlight and good drainage would be a good start for our row crops. I imagined the acre reflecting the primary green of corn and beans, the blue green of chickpeas, and the vibrant green of millet. I took the shovel I was carrying and plunged it into the moist soil at my feet. I set my right foot on and then my left. The shovel with my weight traveled at a slow, steady, satisfying rate. I flipped the clod of precious earth over. We let our knees touch the ground as we bent over the aromatic clod of loamy clay soil.

"That smells good," Lisa sighed.

We looked at each other and smiled. We felt confident about the future but also humbled by the enormous responsibility we were taking on. The spader that my tractor would pull would forever alter this land we were standing on. We had a strong obligation to do right by nature. Mistakes were inevitable but integrity would be essential.

And this was how we built our farm. Each chicken coop, fence line, orchard, and milking barn built by our hands and celebrated as part of a living entity. A living, integrated farm. Some of the buildings are whimsical. Some of the fences meander, and the stanchions in the milking parlor curve to the shape of the cow's neck.

We built our first fence out of manzanita, a scrub that grows throughout California. The woody part of the plant is dense and gnarled. The bark is smooth and apple red. Because not a single branch is straight, the fence undulates with the earth beneath it. What joy, what freedom to build such a fence! We were in heaven. The construction took us weeks. It was very unconventional, and the lack of convention set our imaginations bubbling with other ideas. What type of gate, we wondered, was worthy of such a fence?

The inspired answer was a fulcrum gate, a gate that doesn't swing on hinges but rather moves effortlessly from one balanced point, the fulcrum. We constructed it from larger, thicker, and older manzanita. At the end of the gate is the counterweight. Angle iron that has been blacksmithed into a hook eye moves through a drilled hole on the large beam of the gate. Attached to the iron are whimsical, round clay figures. Together they supply the correct amount of equalizing weight for the gate. When one opens the gate, it feels light as a feather. But it also requires the gate opener to be present, for the gate can quickly get away from you. It needs and draws attention. The art is functional and animated.

*   *   *

Art was always part of my life.

My mother Beverly was an artist. The hands
that held me to her warm breasts, the thumbs that
snapped together my clothes belonged to an exceptional
artist. As a young child I watched her place the oil on
her newly stretched canvas with long, confident strokes,
moving color, form and feeling around the huge eight by
fifteen foot space. She was pulling some visual scene
from memory and sharing it with us. I watched in silence and awe.

When I was growing up Mom would tell us the
story of playing in the corral. While her brother Charles
was happily occupied practicing his lasso on the calves,
she lay with her head resting on a calf's belly, her face
turned to the warm Oklahoma sky. The calf's steady
breath lured her into a meditative muse. She watched
the clouds move by and the dancing of the light between
blue, gray, and white. She watched the dust sparkle in
the bright sun. The scene dazzled her. It marked the
beginning of a life of visual exploration.

Art was always part of this California farm as
well. My mother passed the torch from her creative
hand to mine. My canvas was the soil.

CHAPTER 3

"What the hell was that? " I shout, kicking something that jabs me in the left ankle. I launch the branch in the air with my foot. When it hits the ground, our dog Sydney grabs it with her teeth and brings it to me to throw.

"Marn, it's just a stick!" Lisa replies, trying to control her laughter.

I know she's right, but I can't help but feel like I'm constantly being assaulted by sticks, rocks, bales of hay, tails of cows, and gopher holes on our farm. It's a constant reminder that I cannot see anything to the side of me or below me. I can only view objects that are directly in front of me. An incessant whispering from the cosmos that I am not "the fittest to survive."

"I don't want that stupid stick! It just attacked me!" But I take the stick anyway and throw it for Sydney. I can't resist her doggy smile and enthusiasm.

Yesterday I crossed the creek into the woods to check on the perimeter fencing. Today I will mend it. It's a three-string barbed wire fence we built last year. When wind storms pass through the valley they sometimes push over trees onto the fence. Two weeks ago the wind reached 45 miles per hour. A downed section of fence means loose cattle roaming the county. I didn't want to take any chances.

I love this part of the farm. The woods always feel fresh and free of lingering human movement and chatter. September leaves have newly fallen on the ground. The air is musty. This hillside faces north, and the soil is very different from the flat farmland below. Now I am in the company of black oaks, ponderosa pines and gray pine.

But sweet as it is, when I come here these days I'm constantly fighting back feelings of deep frustration and anger. Seven years ago I could leap over the creek, jog down the hill, or mountain bike up the thin cow trail. Now it takes me 10 minutes just to cross the damn creek. I have to memorize the world around me. First I scan above my head for branches. I turn my head slowly to the sky to see what's there. Now I turn my head down to face my feet.

What's down here? I mutter to myself. I sigh. Many rocks in various shapes and sizes. I stare at them and try to imagine a route that I can take. I make a picture in my mind and timidly take my first step on the projected pathway. Instead of landing on a rock or tree limb, my foot sinks into the creek. Oh well, no time to figure out what went wrong. Instead I keep on the pathway I've created in my mind. To my delight I make it across the creek without another mishap.

My delight quickly changes to annoyance as I am immediately attacked by a branch that escaped my scanning. Luckily I have my trusted Boston Red Sox cap on. Stained with dirt, bark, oil and everything else it has encountered, it faithfully protects my head and eyes. I push aside the branch and pause. Now I can see that the cow path is to my left.

Good. I know that I can follow this easily, for the cows walk with the contour of the land and clear a lot of the brush aside. Sydney is in front of me, leaping back and forth, in and out of my visual field. She has such beautiful agility. I stop and watch her jump from log to rock to a pile of leaves. She exudes a natural confidence that I used to possess.

Directly in front of my eyes is a world easy to perceive. The world beyond my cheekbones and eyebrows is dark and gone. If I turn my head, I can see another little world in front of my nose, but now the tree is lost into total darkness. If the lighting is just right, I may be able to detect a fuzzy, wavy border around my checks and eyebrows.

I am trapped in this narrow place. Trapped in waves of anger, anguish and fear of the eventual darkness that will come to my visual field. The anger is an odd anger. I'm not angry at nature or at some higher being. Instead I am angry at what will happen in the future. I am angry about the emotional pain I will be feeling, not what I'm actually experiencing now. My fear has hardened into anger.

I look at the top of the naked oak. My head is tilted back to its farthest pivot point. The open gesture as the tree branches reach toward the sky moves my mind to a memory of five years ago.

*   *   *

  I was driving my dad into town. We were both hungry for an ice cream cone. My farm was a good twenty minutes outside of town, so the drive gave us some space to just be with each other.

  I stretched out my arm to turn off the radio. *I don't want to hear about sad and horrifying events in Iraq right now,* I thought to myself. *I'll listen to the radio tonight to fill me in on this new war America has entered.* I wanted to have a pleasant drive with my father.

  "Marn, don't you want some water?" my dad asked, with a hint of frustration in his voice. The spring sun had warmed the interior of the car enough that it had made my father thirsty.

  "Sure, it's really hot," I replied, concentrating on the road.

  There was a long pause. Then I could feel Dad nudge my arm. "Here, would you take it already!"

  "What? What are you talking about?"

  "Marney, can't you see that I'm holding the bottle of water right here?" my father said, with fear in his voice. He had been holding the water bottle inches from my right arm that was resting in my lap.

  "No, what bottle of water?"

  "My goodness, Marney, can you see me sitting next to you?"

"No, I *never* can see the person sitting next to me when I drive," I answered, trying to calm my father down.

"Marney, dear, please pull over. I think I should drive."

As I pulled over I was worrying about my dad. He seemed to be overreacting to what to me was just a fact. However, as he questioned me further, I began to realize that something was terribly different about my eyes.

Dad turned the car around, and we came back to the farm. Within minutes I was on the phone making an appointment with an eye doctor. I wasn't worried, but my father and Lisa seemed very concerned.

Before my father had arrived that day, I had spent four hours turning an acre of moist earth. I sat on the tractor feeling the rumbling as the machine and earth worked with and against each other. The sweet smell of the fecund earth made me feel like I was in just the right place. I could see Lisa off in the distance moving the electric cattle fence. I felt like I could happily sit there all day smelling the earth and watching her beautiful body move in the warm spring sun. I loved watching her shoulders lean into and pull the fence posts from the ground. I was feeling blessed.

I was surrounded by joyous things to see. I had no idea that the panic I felt walking in a crowd or the increasing sense of doom I felt approaching the grocery store had anything to do with my eyesight. I thought it was just some silly psychological hang-up I had developed. Hyperventilating while waiting in the checkout line had became routine.

A week later Lisa and I were sitting in the waiting room of a Sacramento eye doctor who specialized in retinal problems. We were tense with fear. Fear of the unknown. In the background, behind the fear, I also felt relief. After this visit I would know what the issue was, and we could both move on from there.

My mind wandered from the People magazine in my lap to the picture I had studied yesterday of the retina. How incredible it is that humans can now draw and photograph the part of our body that meets the light energy from the outside world. The drawing had depicted the beautifully complex surface at the back of the eye. It showed the pathway of the electron and how, with the help of the rod or cone cell, it creates a chemical reaction inside the eye. What amazing beauty we've been able to uncover.

"Marney Blair!" I heard a voice call.

I stood up and both of us went into the office.

The retinal specialist looked into my eyes. He held an instrument in his hand and looked at the back of my eye. Then he shut off the lights in the room and moved a larger instrument in front of my face. It covered both of my eyes and allowed him to examine the retina.

Quickly, without hesitation, he gave his verdict. "You have retinitous pigmentosa. No doubt about it.

There is nothing we can do for you. You will eventually go blind. Every five years, on average, you will lose fifty perfect of your visual field. I suggest that you look into getting a seeing eye dog." He pulled away his instrument and casually walked out of the door.

We sat motionless.

Lisa walked over to where I sat and took my hand. I broke down in tears. I felt completely deflated. All that we had worked toward on the farm was crumbling in front of me. I could not farm blind.

*   *   *

A wind from the west blows my baseball cap off my head. I bend over to pick it up and shift my thoughts to the present. I still have fencing to mend.

"What a shocking time that was," I whisper to the tree. I reach out and touch her solid form, lean into her trunk for support. Then I continue my climb.

Sydney and I reach the fence line and begin to walk along the barrier. She's unhindered by this human construct and darts in and out of the fence to chase a squirrel. I stay on our side of the fence, deep in thought.

The memory of that kind of freedom of movement is buried deep within my muscles. But now I must restrain my movements. I fear the barbed wire that I know is inches from my arm. I cannot see it, but I know that one false move could mean a serious laceration.

I kneel with my weight on one knee as I pull back into shape two strands of wire that have been bowed apart by the daily passage of a fawn or two. I can almost see their bodies moving through as I wrestle the wire back into correct form. The strands now have a consistent space of one foot between them. If the fence is taut and uniform, the cows will stay within their boundaries. But give them the possibility of moving their heads past the plane of the fence into the next ranch, they'll give it a try.

What an interesting illusion the fence really is. A bovine of 1500 pounds can easily bend this fence over and move wherever she pleases. But because the fence is an unnatural human construct, the cow doesn't realize its limitations, at least not until she seizes an opportunity to break the plane of this illusion.

Laughing, I say to the fence, "Thanks for the lesson in metaphors today." The trick is to be like the dog or cow and break beyond these limitations that are really only in my mind. The fences of fear confine my daily movements. The trick to freeing myself from this fear is to be curious like the dog.

Finally I reach the corner post, and Sydney and I start to walk back through the pasture. The openness of the grassy space allows me to relax. I look to the lovely rock outcrop to the north. I can finally let my shoulders down. I breathe deeply and feel less confined, less controlled by my fear of injury. Now I can walk and concern myself with only the changes below my feet.

The blue oak on the other side of the pasture gestures to me with her bowing trunk. I sit with my back leaning on her and feel my mind wander back in time, and I wonder how I made it to such a blessed place.

I had come so far to be here. Fifteen years ago I was weighted down with despair. I had not met Lisa. My mother was dying. My eye disease had not begun to interfere with my vision, but my body was wracked with trauma and weak from too much cerebral laboring. I dressed myself in brown and black and saw the world in shades of gray.

The descent into this dark place took many years of heartache and disappointment. Once I reached the cold, damp bottom, I realized I did not think to carry a single rope to pull me out. Instead, after four years of darkness, a clean new rope came from the warm light above. It was woven from loving friends and teachers. Not being a climber, I had to dedicate myself to learning how to drag myself up and out of that lonely pit.

The exertion was exhausting and, to my delight, also comical and magical. When I finally felt my face on the precious soil above, I cried tears of joy. I looked around at the wonders of an orchard in full bloom, cows grazing in the pasture, a blooming purple iris, and Lisa turning the compost piles.

CHAPTER 4

Growing up in Boulder, Colorado during the early 70s
was like living in Shangri-La. The town is situated just
below a stunning rock formation called the Flatirons in
the foothills of the great Rocky Mountains. One block
from our house was a clear, crisp mountain stream that
whispered its sweet song throughout the city. Boulder
Creek ran cold snow melt, but in the summer we would
brave the swollen creek in inner tubes, laughing our way
downstream as we spun in eddies and bumped into
boulders.

Another creek flowed in the gully at the very
end of our backyard, fed by irrigation runoff from the
University of Colorado's rugby fields. I remember playing in the cold water with my favorite toy, a Fisher Price
house boat. The Flatirons loomed in the distance, and I
could smell a Rocky Mountain spring. I was chugging
my brightly colored Fisher Price boat along the shadowy
banks, the reflections appearing like another dimension.
My daydream was suddenly interrupted by the sound of
Harvey climbing over our fence. He never used the front
door to visit; climbing the fence made more sense to
him. His long black hair, pulled back in a ponytail,
brushed my face as he jumped down next to me.

"Hi," said my friend of few words.

"Hi, Harvey." We sat for a moment in comfortable silence. "Do you wanna play with blocks in my mom's art studio?"

Harvey nodded, and we walked in the warm sun across the backyard, his long strides putting him ahead of me. He was tall and thin. I watched the light warm the rich oils in his Navajo hair. Harvey had a round, open face that was accentuated by his round black-rimmed glasses. The glasses made his black eyes look like magnets that could pull in all kinds of curious things.

I gestured to the low table on the right as we walked into Mom's studio. My brother sat quietly playing with the wooden shapes. Some blocks were already glued together in abstract sculptures. Others were randomly scattered over the table's surface.

My mom walked over to touch Harvey warmly on the shoulder. She made him feel welcome, just like she would any of my friends over the next 25 years. My mother loved people, and they loved her in return. While she rested her hand on Harvey's shoulder, we exchanged a smile. Then she gracefully walked over to the record player and turned up the volume. Silently we built and she painted to the soundtrack of "Hair," the four of us nestled comfortably in the warm studio with its smell of oils, glue, and joy.

Boulder in those days had the kind of grounded, wholesome beauty that I associated with Robert Redford's face. My father and Mr. Redford were both students at the University of Colorado in the 50's. From my eight-year-old perspective, all the men in Boulder looked like Robert Redford and all the women looked like Lindsay Wagner. My mother, on the other hand, had a unique radiance that came from Oklahoma.

We lived across the street from the University. My brother and I would wander freely around the majestic, ivy-covered school grounds. The snapping turtle pond was always on our adventure list for the day. I would lead my brother past the tall sandstone building where my father had studied law to the "wild banks" of the turtle pond. We would play for what seemed like hours. Then I would circle us back to the art studios to find our mom, who was studying painting.

The classroom was filled with busy students. If it was a drawing class, I could see glimpses of their work as they packed up for the day. My mom was always excited to see us and show us all the new exhibits that were in the room next door.

"Look at this, kids! Isn't it amazing how real it looks?" she said one day as she stood over a Duane Hanson sculpture and took in every detail.

"Look how the artist has captured even the hairs on her face!"

The sculpture was a lady dressed in loud clothing, her pose frozen in mid stride. Made of some kind of plastic material, she looked totally alive. It spooked me, but I tried hard to see why my mom found her so exciting.

Art always excited her. She was always busy working on a project. But my mother's love of color did not alleviate the darkness she sought when my father left on business trips. During those times, she retreated to her bedroom, leaving her rosy outlook on the other side of the bedroom door, and drawing the heavy curtains.

When I came home from school, I would open the door to her darkened room to say hi. At the sound of my voice she would sit up in bed.

"Did you have a good day at school?" she would ask, with forced cheer in her voice.

"I did," I'd reply, going to her to get a warm hug. "I don't need anything, Mom. I'm gonna play with Billy," I didn't want to linger. The light after school was perfect for hunting insects.

I walked into my brother's room, "Wanna go to the vacant lot?"

We walked side by side down our street to a lot that wasn't developed, knowing there would be plenty of butterflies and grasshoppers hunting for food in the untamed vegetation. Their feverish activity was infectious, and soon we were kicking up the dirt as we ran to the stream at the back of the lot.

I crouched down near the stream and began looking for ants. I was eager to try a new technique my brother and I had perfected just as we were called into supper the night before. I was certain that we would succeed.

"I got a leaf, Marn!" my brother exclaimed, holding a beautiful twirling maple leaf by the pinnacle. He ran and sat next to where I was watching a parade of ants carry goodies into an anthill. We sat in the cool dirt for awhile, watching the mysterious comings and goings. Then I spotted the ant I wanted.

"Got it!" I held the ant down in the dirt. I was determined this time to send a successful ant raft down the stream to the ocean. The leaf would provide food and shelter for the journey. In previous attempts, the raft would sometimes catch an eddy and sink quickly into the stream. Other times it would get snagged on vegetation. But finally I had learned how to place the raft so it floated gently down the stream. I launched it. The ant was going on a big adventure.

I remember walking home with my brother in the maroon dusk and delicately scented air after one of our evenings of insect hunting. Our strides were perfectly matched. I loved my brother's company. He was a sturdy, lovable teddy bear who was always willing to join my adventures. We were a perfect team.

We walked into the kitchen to find my parents talking quietly. Mom gestured for us to come over to them. Dad said, "Marney, honey, you and Billy will be visiting Oklahoma again this summer. Nana and Ganco will pick you up at the airport in Tulsa." I smiled. I didn't like the intense summer heat in Tulsa, but I loved my grandparents. Maybe this summer I could ride Polly, my great-aunt's horse.

Billy climbed into Dad's lap. I hadn't noticed until now that he was covered with mud and grass stains. He didn't seem to be paying attention to the conversation, but that didn't matter to him. Billy was always game for anything.

"We're going on another adventure, Billy! We're going to Nana and Ganco's again."

"Hooray!" he shouted. He got down from Dad's lap and started jumping up and down. We began to skip out of the room when I caught something out of the corner of my eye. Mom and Dad had closed like a clam around themselves. The conversation had turned serious and adult. I could sense that something had shifted.

CHAPTER 5

"Oh, my sweet, precious angels," Nana sang, holding back tears of joy when my brother and I got off the plane in Tulsa. She enveloped us in her velvety warmth.

My grandfather stood to the side, letting Agnes make a fuss over us before embracing us with an athletic hug. Even in the heat of summer Ganco had his dapper hat on. He always looked so handsome.

Tulsa was a world away from my home in Boulder. Boulder was an old mining town turned chic. The crusty old saloons were now packed with engineers, poets and football players letting off steam from their studies at CU. The city my grandparents lived in and where my mom grew up was still grounded in work that involved the land and the hand. In Tulsa times were good, but every hand still had the calluses of the Great Depression. And the land, this flat barren place, was their savior.

The town was also full of adoring relatives. As soon as Nana opened the door of their duplex the phone started ringing.

"Marney, honey, it's your granny. She wants to welcome you home," Nana said, then continued talking on the phone. "Yes, Mother. Yes, Mother. Yes, Mother. We'll come over tomorrow."

Nana handed me the phone. "Hi, Granny," I greeted her shyly. Even though she was my great grandmother, I didn't really know her. She wasn't like my mother or Nana. There was always something in her tone that indicated that she wanted something. My mother and grandmother always made sure their love preceded their words. Granny's tone suggested that her love came with conditions.

I spoke to Granny for a minute and then heard screams of excitement from the living room.

"Where are those angels?" I just gotta squeeze them, hmm hmm lord!" came a woman's voice from the freezing cold, air-conditioned living room.

"Is that Mildred?" Granny barked through the phone.

I was too rattled to reply. Fortunately my great aunt Mildred took the phone from my hand. I stepped aside, only to be grabbed lovingly by her white, jewel-adorned hand.

"Mother ......" The conversation drifted out of my consciousness, but I couldn't escape Mildred's love hold.

"Well, Agnes, it looks like Mother wants all of us to come over right now," Mildred exclaimed with disappointment. "Agnes, did you hear me, darling?"

My grandmother was sitting in front of her favorite show, "As the World Turns," and hadn't heard a word her little sister was saying. I figured that she was resigning herself to being controlled by her younger sister and mother today. I knew not to worry, however, because our trip to the Arkansas farm was only a week away, and there we always had Nana and Ganco to ourselves.

Mildred, her husband Bill, Nana, my brother and I loaded ourselves into the very cold Cadillac. My Uncle Bill didn't say a word as he drove us through the flat, sparsely populated countryside to my great-grandparent's house. Nana and Mildred showered Billy and me with compliments, Nana holding my hand with loving devotion. She and Mildred started talking up a storm regarding family matters, and I drifted into a meditative state.

Nana's laser-like transmission of love would become familiar to me. It was the same type of concentrated emotion that my mom shared with me over the years. Nana could deliver this stream of love through her palms and through her chocolate brown eyes. My mom delivered the same warm love stream through her voice, her hugs, and her art.

Paw Paw, my great grandfather, was just returning from the cow pastures when we pulled in. He picked up his pace when he saw that his great grandkids from Colorado were inside. My heart swelled. I loved him from the depths of my DNA. Billy and I walked toward him, suddenly feeling a bit shy, and took turns embracing his damp, sweet-smelling torso. The aroma of tobacco, honey, and black soil filled my nostrils and calmed my young soul. The smell was familiar beyond my years.

The farm was like so many in Oklahoma, a modest acreage that could support cattle, chickens, vegetable production and honeybees. Except for grains, the ingredients for every meal came from this land.

We all walked into the house and said hello to Granny. The house was cold from the air conditioner, and the curtains were drawn. The sound of newborn chicks filled the living room. I could sense the swirling tension of the various personalities in the modest farmhouse. I wasn't used to so many family members. It felt overwhelming. In an act of self- preservation my brother and I focused on the busy box of day-old chicks placed next to Granny's rocker.

I knew that Granny was the queen bee of this clan, but the maze of personalities was hard to negotiate without the aid of my mother. I felt loved and cared for, but the culture of Oklahoma was wildly different from my Colorado home. I was like a little hatchling trying to understand southern culture and the bizarre world of extended family.

At the age of eight it didn't occur to me to question why I was out of contact with my mother for four weeks. I spoke on the phone with her only once the entire time. As I learned when I was older, my father kept us in the dark in order to protect us from the pain. The truth was that Beverly didn't call me because she was emotionally incapable of motherhood during the summer. The long summer days left her manic and eventually spent and depressed. Our father sent us to Tulsa to shelter us from the emotional roller coaster. There would be more summers like this. I'm grateful that I was spared her anguish and instead got to enjoy summers with my relatives.

My Nana grew up on an Oklahoma truck farm with three sisters and two brothers. Each of them found ways to survive the Great Depression. Some of my great aunts made the trek to California to build warships in Oakland. After the war they came back home to Tulsa.

By the time I was eating their fried okra they all lived comfortable, middle-class lives. The women worked hard to leave behind the dust and grind of farm life. Their men performed in rodeos and took their cattle to auction yards. They always had tanned faces up to their brows, their foreheads remaining pearly white under the brim of their cowboy hats.

That afternoon at Granny and Paw Paw's, we all ate fried okra, fresh tomatoes, fried chicken, and collards. The men went outside after lunch and sat under an old oak, where Paw Paw smoked his pipe. Billy and I were trapped inside with the big Zenith in the corner flashing images of "The Price is Right."

Finally we loaded back into Uncle Bill's car and rode back to Tulsa. Despite being filled to the brim with antiques, my Nana's house felt calm and uncluttered in comparison. I felt as if I could finally relax. I think Nana felt the same way. She went into the kitchen and baked us a velvet chocolate cake, her love for us traveling down the spoon and into the thick, rich batter.

That night I slept in Nana's room. The familiar bed was surrounded by strange racks of clothes still with tags, bins of shoes, tables of perfume bottles, and boxes of hats. It wasn't messy, for everything had its place on the rack or neatly stacked against a wall.

I climbed into her comfy bed and looked at my mother looming large above me. Her life size portrait captured her as the football queen of Will Rogers High School. She wore a gold cape over an elaborate gold dress. On her head was a gold crown dappled with jewels. She looked straight at me. I thought I could see sadness in her eyes, but no one else in the family agreed with me. Beverly was the real queen—real royalty—for football was the only game in town.

I said goodnight to my mother and slept, comforted by her portrait and the knowledge that this Oklahoma clan adored her.

I rose before dawn to the sound of Ganco humming in the kitchen. I adored this time of day because it always seemed to give clues as to what might happen in the hours to come. My brother was like my grandmother and chose to sleep until the sun reached over the tops of the trees.

Not today, however. Ganco and I were bubbling with excitement. This morning all of us would be driving to the Ozark Mountains in Arkansas where Ganco and Nana had a retirement farm. The task of rousing my grandmother and brother at this early hour was daunting, but we were energized by the prospect of seeing the big city of Tulsa disappear in our rear view mirror.

"Agnes, come on, honey. Get up," my grandfather coaxed, nudging Nana from her deep, deep sleep. Suddenly her left leg swung out from the covers and pushed Ganco away. He and I looked at each other and laughed. He nudged her again. This time she rolled over, grunted, and pulled a pillow over her head.

"Come on, Marney. We'll pack the car and then we can ask Billy to get Agnes up," said Ganco, with a tone that suggested he knew the exact strategy to get Nana out of bed.

Later, as we drove away from Tulsa with sleepy Nana and Billy cuddling in the back seat, I felt a deep sense of freedom and happiness. We were leaving the world of human drama for the freedom you can only find in nature. We were entering a world that felt just right to me. A place of land and animals.

As my grandparents' mobile home came into view, I could see the goats frolicking in the tall fescue near Adam's house. He was the caretaker of my grandfather's farm. I liked Adam but feared the billy goat that would often chase Billy and me down the road.

Before pulling into the driveway, Ganco stopped at a small gray shack. It was the spring house.

"Come on, Billy and Marney," he said, as he grabbed a large stick by the side of the shack.

He slowly opened the door.

"Now stand back and I'll remove all the tarantulas."

My brother and I stood in the dark doorway as my grandfather lifted the board that covered the cold spring. I wasn't really scared, for I fully trusted Ganco, but rather was amazed at the spiders' willingness to challenge this large human.

Whap.

Whap. Whap.

He killed five spiders on the spot. The others fled between the wall slats to find shelter in the grass outside.

"Well, that's good. Now come here and look at this beautiful water," he beckoned. The spring was pillowed by glowing watercress growing in the daylight that filtered through the slats. We could feel the vibrant life bubbling from this hole in the ground. This was the water we would drink while we stayed at the farm. How lucky we were.

Ganco was proud of his farm—all the fences he had built, the fescue he tended, and the herd he had selected—and he took great pleasure in sharing it with all of his grandkids.

"Look!" he pointed. "Here's the spot where we'll build the swimming pool. It'll start here and go to this spot. Then the water from the spring will fill at the north end and exit here on this southern point," he explained, with the confidence of a man who still did 60 push-ups and 150 sit-ups every morning. "Just think how fun it'll be to swim in a cool, spring-fed pool!"

We stepped outside of the shack and looked off into the open countryside. I could see black angus cows moving in the pasture by the mobile home. Off to the right was forest land that swept down to the river. The curve of the hills created a soft, moist light. I stood next to my brother and grandfather, feeling safe in the generous arms of the Ozarks and awed by her abundant beauty. I knew that I'd be fine without my mother this summer.

CHAPTER 6

The harmony in Boulder was shattered in the spring of 1972. It happened the moment the cops threw tear gas at the students running across our front lawn. I was ten that spring and stood at the living room window watching the splashes of color rushing past. Everything was moving too fast to focus on a person. You could feel the hot air of anger rippling through the neighborhood. Violence was unfamiliar to me. I was confused, disoriented, and scared.

Our neighbor down the road came out with a glass of whiskey in his hand to see what all the commotion was about. Without warning, the students turned and swarmed him like a hive of angry bees on his suburban lawn. Suddenly riot cops were circling around them, their clubs waving in the air.

Whack!

Our neighbor went down, blood oozing from his head. His injury changed his life forever. He would never speak again.

My life changed that spring as well. I had witnessed violence and destruction first-hand, and I knew that no Bionic Woman or other superhero could make this right. No longer would my brother and I wander freely to see the turtles, to buy candy at the drugstore, or to play tag on the church lawn.

When IBM, the company my father worked for, transferred him to Mexico City three years later, it felt like we were escaping a country under siege. Our family had no idea what adventures lay ahead, but my mother and father felt that it was an important and timely departure.

I was in fifth grade and my brother was in second. Every school day we would take a thirty-minute bus ride to our new school. The bus drove along the boulevard of Chapultepec Park with its huge tropical trees and brilliant tiled sculptures. The giant sculptures of stone faces, ancient Aztec relics, were much older than the trees. The lush greens and brown dirt soothed my eyes, and I could feel the anxiety of living in a mega city leaving my body and being absorbed and transformed by the large palm trees.

The bus climbed to a rise in the urban park and I could see the enormous city in front of me, an unnatural congestion of souls packed on this old Aztec city. I could feel every breath of desperation. Flashes of armless children, eye-less mothers, frothing men and mangy dogs stormed around in my brain. I missed the trees. I missed the sanity of the trees. The symmetry. This light traveled on a wavelength of uncluttered purity.

"Thank you, trees," I said to myself.

After school Mom and I would go to the mercado for our fresh fruits and vegetables. Some days I could convince her to stop at the pasteleria to get some delicious bollos, a type of sweet bread buns. We walked to the market pulling our carts that we would fill with food in pinks, reds, greens, yellows, and beige. What beauty! The abundance of fresh food was life affirming.

The weekends in Mexico were our time to travel beyond the city limits. This took hours because this was the largest city in the world. During these weekends our family would see the most glorious landscape rolling like waves past our car windows. Sometimes it was dense tropical vegetation with leaves as large as our car door. The birds spoke in constant cheery chatter. Other times the landscape was open and dry, full of cacti and grass huts. Beauty was in the space and pauses. Large, spiny, blue-green iguanas would lounge on fallen vegetation by the roadside. The less fortunate ones would be hanging by their tails as some of the villagers carried them home for dinner.

I felt good here. I felt safe here with my family.

I was too young to recognize it, but I experienced two very different worlds in Mexico. On weekends when the family would journey outside of the metropolis, I felt embraced by the country's beauty. The exotic deserts and the dripping jungles reinforced my growing sense of the sanity inherent in the natural world. Here in these small, ancient villages the people worked within the landscape. The color of their skin, the texture of their clothes, even the sound of their laughter complemented the landscape. The people and the land were one. The boy holding the iguana for sale by the roadside came into view as if he had precipitated out of a palette of oil paints. He was of this land, I imagined roots growing from his feet.

Life in the city felt quite different.

In Mexico there's no middle class, so IBM rented us a three-story mansion with huge doors and a central staircase made of mahogany, stained glass windows, and separate quarters for the maids. We had rooms we called "the piano room" and "the stereo room." My brother had two bedrooms. One was an upstairs apartment complete with its own balconies, kitchen, and bath. Downstairs he had a bedroom across the large hall from mine.

The wood in the house was warm, but the beautiful tiles that lined the floors always carried a chill. In the middle of the second floor was the TV room where I would sit in our brown beanbag chair every week watching "The Carol Burnett Show" on the Zenith TV.

Behind the TV room were my parents' bedroom and my mother's art studio. Her studio was very different from the one we left behind in Boulder. There crisp, penetrating alpine colors filled my mother's canvases. Her studio here was filled with green and magenta light from the lush vegetation, and she had a dreamy view of our fig tree and a five-story wall of bougainvillea.

At times my mother was very happy in this room. In the middle was a sturdy, waist-high art table that her father had built for her. The top slid back so that she could store her paintings flat inside. I loved to rush upstairs after school to find her contemplating her latest project. She would be standing there in her own golden light, her face electric with ideas.

Other times she was not happy.

My parent's bedroom had heavy curtains. Most days my mother would open them to let in the spirit of the day. But on other days, she wanted to keep everything out, including us. Far too often, I would run up the stairs after school with exciting news about my day and find her in darkness.

My room faced Arquimedes Street, a three-lane boulevard. I would look out the window and watch a variety of people carry on with their lives. I might see a man with a donkey carrying brooms or, further up the street, a band of boys in school uniforms teasing one of their friends. Eventually bored, I'd walk over to my bed and turn on my banana yellow AM/FM radio. The radio dial never moved from my favorite station. It played The Beatles twenty-four hours a day.

The fall season moved day by day as my family learned the language and customs of this remarkable land. We each had our struggles and bouts of loneliness. Then, as the sun passed closer to her lowest marker, my grandparents announced that they would make the journey to Mexico to join us for Christmas. My mother and father were amazed by their courage and generosity.

The day they arrived my mother took us to the huge open air market, Mercado de la Merced. I watched Nana looking at jewelry, the gold reflected in her eyes. Her beautiful face was lit up like she was a ten-year-old in a bin full of puppies. Although she didn't know a word of Spanish, she was managing to chat and laugh with the vendor like he was an old friend. She motioned me over.

"Marney, honey, come look at this precious heart necklace. Isn't it sweet? Would you like to have it, honey?"

It looked hideous and gaudy to me, and it probably wasn't even real gold. I was about to tell her so but stopped when I looked into her velvety black eyes. Her excitement warmed my heart.

"I'm not quite sure, Nana," I said gently, not wanting to hurt her feelings.

"Honey, I want to give it to you." Before I knew it, I had the necklace hanging weightlessly on my chest.

Behind me the Mercado de la Merced buzzed with commerce. This was the place to be on Saturday. My mother and brother were at a stall looking at toys. They were standing in front of a display of elaborate kits, and I knew that eventually my mother would give in.

My grandmother and grandfather spent the entire month of December with us. The piano room was filled with gifts from the States, and the kitchen was filling up with cakes and cookies that Nana was busy baking. Her Martha Washington chocolate cake sat on a stand glistening with fat and sugar that Nana had whipped by hand.

My grandmother spoke with anyone who would listen. She didn't care if they understood her (she didn't speak any Spanish). Her *joie de vivre* was to be close to people every day. She loved people, and peopled loved her.

One afternoon I walked around the corner to the Sugar Shack, a corner sweet shop, where I was hoping to find my brother and grandmother. Before I could see anyone inside the tiny storefront, I felt Nana's warmth waft out the door like a breeze. She was sitting on a stool, one leg swinging back and forth to an internal tune, and chatting with the shopkeeper. Billy and his friend Bobbie were playing jacks on the floor nearby. They were cushioned by colorful packages of candy. Billy had jacks in one hand ready for a throw and in the other a big stick of chewing gum.

I wanted sugar, too, and a big hug from my grandmother. I walked over to her and she held me tight, filling me up with her love.

I was happy to be with my grandmother and proud of her ability to light up a room. She possessed a kind of liberation from worry. Every soul she met, she assumed was a good, loving person. I was more cautious, like my father's side of the family.

I bought a chocolate bar and went over to watch the game of jacks. Bobby gave me a quick smile and went back to concentrating on the game. I stroked Billy's blond hair. He absorbed it like a puppy.

When I became bored with the game, I hugged my grandmother goodbye.

"Billy, make sure to come home before dark," I called, as I walked out onto the tree-lined street. Now that the heat of the day was passing, I could feel the city of millions waking up from the siesta hour. I could hear kids on the next block playing soccer.

I walked home and went up to my bedroom to read. I stood at the window and looked out at the vast city humming with human activity. Cars raced down the boulevard below. People walked north and south along the maze of sidewalks. I peered into the trees. The sky was dotted with light, whimsical clouds. I pulled up my white chair and watched. I liked the clouds. I liked my own company. I liked sitting, watching and absorbing the remaining light of the day.

CHAPTER 7

Just as my eyes, nose and ears began to adjust to the enormity of Mexico City, we were packing our clothes and moving back to the States. My father's assignment for IBM had ended, and the family began imagining our lives in New York State.

One day in 1976 I found myself surrounded by large green maple and oak leaves. Dark gray bark reflected the mood of the drippy forest of Westchester County. The openness of the Mexican high plateau had been replaced by dense forest.

My science teacher, Mr. Steele, was taking our seventh grade class to the woods behind Fox Lane Middle School. He had given each of us a small plot to study with a partner. The class exploded out the back door, hungry for an adventure. This area of wilds behind the school was usually off-limits to students. Now Mr. Steele was giving us permission to study it. I was delighted—the mystery of the dark woods would soon be revealed.

Keith was my designated partner. I had never spoken to him before, but my grandmother had taught me to welcome every chance to meet a new person. Luckily, Keith was shy and quiet, so we could observe without too much unnecessary talking.

This was to be our little world for the next 15 weeks! The plots were marked by string that created five-foot squares. Keith and I chose a plot that had a large oak tree. Our mission was to monitor all activity in this world. We started with the plants because they were so abundant. We were to catalog every tree, bush, flower, and grass, insects and mammals.

My homework that night was to make a chart to record our observations. After dinner my mother and I chatted about the day over a warm glass of milk and homemade ginger snaps. Then I scampered up the wooden staircase to my room.

I loved to study in my room. I had my own stereo, and I could gaze out at the tops of the oak and maple trees. In Mexico City, the room always seemed filled with sounds of the metropolis below. Here in my new home I felt like I was in a tree house.

I carefully drew my chart, making a column for listing the living things I would see or anticipated seeing. Each visit to the plot I would make a new chart. This chart would allow me to record the daily living activity of my plot. I worked well past my bedtime. I was too excited to sleep. I read about spiders and why they build webs. I read about how a maple grows from its seed.

I was thrilled with the idea that I could study these woods. While I lived in Mexico and Boulder I found Mother Nature always enticing me to enter her world. But I never had a road map to discover her secrets. Now it felt like I was being offered a doorway. I was being given a chance to do more than just play but rather to understand nature's inner workings.

I wanted to tangle in the weavings of life.

The doorway opened with little fanfare. Mr. Steele simply introduced the idea of science to me. I couldn't believe my good fortune. An entire system had been developed to explore what I had been longing to understand.

The next day I found out that my partner had watched "Happy Days" instead of making his chart. Several of my classmates gathered around him, laughing as they recalled the entire episode. Anxious to get back to the woods, I ignored them. Instead I daydreamed about spiders, maple leaves, earthworms, and mushrooms.

As our class crossed the dark brook and scrambled up the hillside, I took in the sweet smell of decaying leaves. The ground was spongy, and I lingered behind to look at a bright red mushroom. I got on my hands and knees and looked closely at its stem.

I found my plot when I caught up with the class. I could hear the clamor in the background as other students looked for theirs. As soon as I stepped into the twine square, I began looking in earnest for the spider I had seen the day before and the mushroom that I knew would be there. My eyes locked on my mushroom friend, and the natural world instantly drew me in. I was living now among the tiny insects and plants.

Keith jumped into our plot and startled me.

"Whatta ya lookin' at?"

"A cool black millipede," I replied, bubbling with excitement.

He settled down in the plot, and we began to fill out the chart I had made. Next we took the ball of string Mr. Steele had given us and made a grid that produced four quadrants.

I got on my hands and knees and looked closely at a leaf.

"I know from its lobes it must be an oak leaf," I proclaimed proudly, for I recognized the shape from the encyclopedia I was reading the night before.

Keith took the compass to find out the leaf's location.

"It's in the north corner of the plot," he declared.

I entered "oak leaf "in the column under "deciduous trees" and marked that it was in the N quadrant. Our first entry! This was going to be so cool.

Keith jumped out of the plot and skipped up the hill to throw a stick at John.

I knew then that it was up to me to map and describe this miniature world. That was fine with me. I liked working alone and didn't want to be distracted by a person jumping in and out of this little world.

Over the following days, I would sit and draw the plants that I observed. Then I would go back to the classroom to find out what they were. I was surprised to learn that many people before me had spent lifetimes cataloguing the very things I was finding in my treasure hunt. The botany book was filled with vivid descriptions of the seeds, flowers, roots and leaves of each plant.

My passion for research blossomed. How wonderful it was to journey into the world of books and find answers to seemingly complex questions, such as the name of the majestic tree I was seeing. Then there were the intriguing pictures of cell division, photosynthesis, and fluid transport. I had entered a world of mysteries to explore.

After our class mapped all of the vegetation, we began on the insect and animal world. This world was even more dynamic and exciting. It moved and changed. It told stories, like why the spider chose to build her web in a particular place, or how the salamander built its den. Nature was beginning to make sense, now that I had found a doorway into this world.

By the time I stepped into Mr. Kluge's Earth Science class in my senior year in High School, I pictured myself in a white lab coat. I knew I wanted to be a scientist. We studied things that we could see only in our imaginations. We hovered above the earth and imagined how the movement of water created such wonderful works of art on land. We went below the earth and imagined the heat building and the eventual explosion that would create the volcanoes. The teacher gave us a tool box of scientific laws and theories that would help me wherever I wanted to travel.

One chilly fall day, I arrived home from school to find Beverly sitting in the kitchen reading *Art in America*. A warm pot of Red Zinger tea sat on the table in anticipation of my arrival.

"Mom, we studied the coolest stuff in school today," I said, as I burst into the kitchen.

"Here, have a cup of tea and tell me about it. I just made it," she replied with a smile, setting down her magazine.

"The earth is in constant motion. Plates of the earth move and at times they subduct another plate to cause a rising, like in California. Other times the earth's crust can crash into itself, like the Himalayas and India. And rivers move and meander, too. We saw these cool pictures today of the rivers and how over time they create ox bows, islands, new channels. All sorts of things." Mom let me gush on, then shared some of her own enthusiasm.

"Look at these pictures of Cristo's new work," she said, pointing to the photos in her magazine. "He's working with similar concepts. He's illustrating the ideas of how landscape is in motion, how landscape is art."

We talked for over an hour, exchanging thoughts about the earth and her beauty. I explained the science of movement. She explained the art of shadow and light. My head whirled with these concepts and ideas.

Later that fall I would find my mother in her studio when I returned home from school. I'd pull up a chair next to her art table. The pot of tea would be sitting on a shelf along with her vases filled with brushes, open tubes of paint and stacks of art books.

On the art table was a hot glue gun and lots of carefully torn pieces of paper. Some of the paper was colored using pastels. Thick strips of paper had been glued together to reveal a three-dimensional paper sculpture.

I looked in awe at this work in progress. My mother, over the course of months, had been synthesizing our earth conversations into art forms. She had manipulated the strips of paper into flowing contours that suggested a bird's-eye view of the Andes. The small two-by-two-foot sculpture was fragile yet sturdy, still yet in motion.

The summer after my graduation from high school, Darwin, our Australian sheepdog, was my faithful guide into the dark moist woods. Every weekend we would set out to explore the Pound Ridge Reservation in Westchester, New York. I would start up the 1970 gray station wagon that my parents bought in Okmulgee, Oklahoma. It was a huge but cozy car, with a cool eight-track tape player.

On the trail Darwin would run ahead of me with boundless energy. He would then run back and circle in front of me, nose to the ground. Then he would be off again to scout the next 300 feet of trail. I loved this rhythm. The walks were never a linear experience but a loping back and forth, as if we were knitting a fabric of our experience for the day. If Darwin had a string of yarn attached to his collar, he would have woven a beautiful blanket.

I was in a living laboratory. We would splash through streams to find frogs and spiders jumping. I would turn over rocks to find millipedes and centipedes. High above my head was the constant movement of the tree limbs with their radiant leaves. Below my feet was a moist world inhabited by ants, worms, and salamanders. I could often hear Mr. Steele's voice in my head, explaining a concept or pointing out the metamorphic rocks that he had taught us to identify.

Darwin had an incredible way about him. If something caught his interest, he would pursue it without hesitation. Each smell would lead to another discovery. He was always in pursuit of experiences, without stopping for contemplation.

I, on the other hand, was very contemplative. I would see a beautiful mauve leaf and my mind would wander to memories of warm Sunday breakfasts. Then my mind would ponder the leaf's color and wonder why this particular shade. Then, finally, I would find myself resisting picking up the leaf. *Best to leave the leaf there,* I would say to myself.

Without fail, I would end up reciting my teenage mantra. "What is life? What is the meaning of life? Why am I here?" I would pose to Darwin.

I never seemed to get anywhere with these questions, in part because my companion was uninterested in debating them. He would just look at me adoringly and run ahead on the path.

Many mornings, after breakfast with my parents and brother, I would pack my backpack with water, a smoked turkey sandwich with muenster cheese, and on occasion, my very special book, *The Tao Te Ching* by Lao Tsu and translated by Gia-Fu Feng and Jane English. The book featured wonderful landscape pictures taken by Jane English alongside ancient Chinese teachings. I would rest from my exploring and draw out this book from my pack.

I loved this book for two reasons. First my dear friend Tom gave it to me. Tom was a handsome, nerdy guy, who was the best camping companion I had ever been with. He was an Eagle Scout who had everything one would need in a pack, and he had boundless energy. He saw the natural world as a playground, as a place to discover oneself through challenge and adventure. I admired this perspective. I saw this book as a connection to Tom and Tom's world.

I loved this book, too, for what I didn't understand in its simple but elusive poetry. Although it seemed to be beyond what the human heart and mind could really comprehend, I knew it was ancient and wise. And, sometimes, there would come a fleeting moment of comprehension.

During the week after school, I would gaze at the pictures. Occasionally I would read the poetry. It was very hard to understand.

Tao Te Ching

Chapter 43

The softest thing in the universe
Overcomes the hardest thing in the universe.
That without substance can enter where there is no room.
Here I know the value of non-action.

Teaching without words and work without doing
Are understood by very few.

translated by Gia-fu Feng and Jane English

The MetroNorth commuter line hammered through the dense Westchester County forest. I could feel the contrast of moods. My mother and I were headed to New York City for adventure. The rest of the car's sleepy passengers were headed to their 9 to 5 jobs.

The train wove through little hamlets like Chappaqua and Bedford Hills. As we churned closer to Manhattan it straightened, dove into tunnels, and gained speed. The intensified click-clack quickened my heart rate. I turned to my mother. "I can feel it! We're almost there!"

"We're about twenty minutes from Grand Central Station. We should start getting ready," Beverly replied. She stood and grabbed her briefcase. It was full of issues of the *Gallery Guide* and *Art in America* and *The New York Times Arts and Leisure* section.

We joined the rest of the commuters, poised like racers in the starting blocks. Soon we would become a wave of people spilling into one underground building, most of us scrambling to get to their small corner in this vast island. Although my mother and I were on a different mission, we couldn't dawdle or we would be trampled once the train doors opened.

Throughout my high school years, Beverly taught me all about the current issues in visual art. New

York was the center for art in the late seventies and eighties, and we spent many hours in this living classroom.

She was fascinated by light and color. Although she played with texture and shapes, she never found them as alluring as the dancing light and the inexhaustible mixtures and interplay of colors. Her energy for the pursuit of this mystery seemed limitless. Some of my fondest memories of my mother are our trips to Manhattan through the cold rain searching for obscure galleries. I was mainly interested in the exotic food that we would encounter, as we always ate well on these adventures. My mother, on the other hand, was looking for nourishment in new and exciting visual art.

The train pulled into Grand Central. Beverly grabbed my hand firmly and we rushed with the current. She was no longer an Okie from Tulsa but a lioness on the hunt, graceful, excited, and focused on her target.

As usual, my first target was a sweet treat.

"Mom, look at those yummy bagels," I said, as we walked by the pastry shop Zabars.

"Now look, Marn, you just had…. Hmmm. I guess I could go for one of *those*," she replied, pointing to the chocolate croissants that had just caught her eye.

We stood outside the bakery for a moment, admiring the bagels, giant muffins, sweet rolls, Kaiser rolls, and Danish piled high on the counters. The bakers barked at the patrons to hurry and make a decision.

Commuters whizzed by us, weaving in and out. The aroma of rich, dark coffee was giving me a contact high.

I turned to say something to my mom, but she had already joined the line at the counter. She confidently shouted out her order.

Amazing, I smiled to myself. She had learned the art of crowds from the mercado in Mexico City. The shy football queen from Tulsa could now out-muscle the business suit next to her. She had come into her own power as a woman. She was gorgeous.

With treats in hand, we descended into the NYC subway. The warm, dank air plastered itself to my face. It was filled with the smell of humans and machines. The subway took us to Spring Street in lower Manhattan.

As we walked with the crowd up the subway stairs, I was taken by the city's size and sophistication. Everything seemed orderly and larger than human scale. Even the sidewalks were super-sized to accommodate the hordes of people who used them every day. The commerce of the world happened here on this tiny island.

I looked down at my mom's hand clutching the *Gallery Guide*. It might as well have been named the Gallery *Bible*, for we didn't venture anywhere that wasn't mentioned in this weekly artists' publication.

Off in the distance I could see our first destination. An art gallery banner billowed two stories high, its bright colors in stark contrast to the black and gray grime of the street. We walked with determination, swerving left and right to avoid trash cans, drug addicts, and vomit from the previous night. We took a narrow elevator up to the seventh floor and walked into a sea of deep, deep reds.

Julian Schnabel's reds were so delicious I could almost taste their velvety warmth. I wandered through the gallery, gazing at each inviting work. Occasionally I would catch a glimpse of the gray, damp world outside on Bleeker Street and feel grateful to be surrounded by the warm reds.

It was an incredibly exciting time in SoHo. My mom had sniffed it out on her own, long before it had been discovered by the masses. The streets were filled with homeless people and some hardened souls who liked the life in such an intense neighborhood. It was this dirty harshness that made the art so marvelous.

My mother could channel the muse and magically pick just the right galleries for us to visit. I saw works by David Salle, Cindy Sherman, and Susan Rothenberg. My mother would stand in front of a work for awhile and then begin to explain to me the unique perspective that each artist was trying to share with the world. She opened doors for me.

I was beginning to see life from two very different perspectives. As a burgeoning scientist, my mind was being trained to set aside my perceptions of nature and test only what could be measured quantitatively. In order to study the spider in the woods, for example, I must learn how to chart its movements by collecting data. But this world of art was a different exploration of nature. The artists were trying to convey as truthfully as they could their perception of the world as they experienced it. For example, Cindy Sherman's self portraits had underlying political messages, but her main goal seemed to be to show how she perceived the images associated with fairy tales. Her art was gritty, humorous, and alluring. On a whole, it seemed that artists were exaggerating and exploring visual ideas in nature.

After eight hours in the city, my mother and I would board the train back to the sleepy town of Bedford. I would close my eyes to remember the art I had seen and would find images shining in my mind's eye.

Light.

Every visual artist works with the ways in which the energy of light impacts the eyes of the viewer. My mother showed me that color and textures are all felt by my eyes.

I was lucky to have this experience of visual art at a young age. It recontoured my emotional rivers, giving my teenage angst new outlets, eddies, and deltas. When my life felt like it was full of turbulence, a piece of art could calm my emotional currents to a babbling brook. Color had a wave of feeling behind it. It was not contrived. I was training my heart and soul to swim these subtle waters. I could feel the turmoil of Van Gogh and then the sublime tranquility of Monet. The paintings became my close friends.

For example, there was Mark Rothko.

I saw his work for the first time in New York City. The painting had a maroon that levitated off the canvas toward me. I briefly felt as if my feet were leaving the ground. It was sublime. Quickly the moment passed, and I was back in the crowded gallery negotiating people.

But the maroon stayed with me.

Another painter I turned to for comfort I was able to see in person.

Helen Frankenthaler was wearing a gorgeous scarf around her neck as she walked toward the MOMA escalator. I couldn't help but notice her wonderfully confident posture as she descended out of sight. Frankenthaler's work in the MOMA was bold in its simple beauty. The paint was allowed to bleed into the canvas and create a living landscape. Later, in my mind, I would travel back to her bleeding colors to feel the texture and interplay of the colorful world we live in. It was emotionally honest. Frankenthaler's bold honesty still gives me strength to engage in the natural world around me.

Two years later, after visiting galleries with my mom dozens of times, I learned that creative, inspirational light wasn't reserved for just the artist. Rather, it was a normal function of the natural world. My insight came during a trip to Europe with my brother when I was eighteen and he was sixteen.

As we stepped off the train in Southern France, I could immediately sense that the light there was different. My brother and I had traveled a long and hilarious journey from Paris aboard a bullet train the night before. I felt rather smug because we had begun to master the Eurorail experience and had survived the Paris train station. Neither of us knew French, and it was a miracle that we got on the correct train.

In Paris, Billy and I had amused ourselves by buying a bottle of wine, along with bread, cheese and some yummy cured meat. We stuffed our faces as the train rushed through the French countryside. The train was showing a French-dubbed version of *The Sound of Music*. Everything struck us as amusing.

The train arrived in Avignon in the afternoon, under a brilliant, moist summer sun. My brother and I walked around in a daze. Neither of us could articulate what we were seeing. There was something about the light. The French light. Finally we began to talk about the "quality" of light, and we were able to name what we saw.

Cezanne was everywhere. It was unmistakable.

Over the years our mother had gently opened our eyes. Just as great artists were able to capture the feeling behind the light here, we had learned to experience this different quality of light. It had a certain warmth that was distinctive and incredibly familiar.

I'll save these images to enjoy later, I said to myself, as the light danced around me. I knew that I would call upon them later. For the rest of our trip, I was busy distilling the essence of each region and filing it away.

In Madrid, my brother and I attended a bullfight. Perched high above the ring, I watched the colors dance before my eyes in the one hundred degree heat. After considerable fanfare, the most gorgeous man I had ever seen walked into the ring. The matador. I took a deep breath, transfixed by the beauty before me.

His red cape billowed in the wind. The quality of that red in the light was mesmerizing. It was an archetypal red, a color that goes to your core. A red so beguiling that by the time the bull met his "maker," the streams of blood squirting from his neck were strangely within context of the entire sensory-filled day. *This*, I told myself, is a Spanish red.

That night, sweating in my pension in Madrid, I imagined my eyes as organs of digestion. The eyes take these wonderful gifts from nature and transform them into chemicals through a process of digestion. I eat what I see and it becomes a part of me. In fact, I thought, gazing up at the ceiling, isn't this what a leaf does? She creates sugars; I create neuro-transmitters.

After a month in Europe, Billy and I returned to Bedford, where I found a letter from the University of California, San Diego waiting for me. I ran through the house screaming with joy. I was going to study science in California!

I watched the sun rise later each day, knowing that when fall arrived I would leave New York. I pulled

my Norwegian leather backpack down from the closet
and carefully filled it with treasured items. First to fit
nicely in the heart of the pack was *The Tao Te Ching*. I slid
five postcards in the Taoist book: Susan Rothenberg's
"Horse" painting, Laurie Anderson with her violin,
Mark Rothko's maroon painting, Cezanne's "Still Life,"
and Steglitz's portrait of O'Keeffe. The last item to fit
comfortably into my pack was a small sculpture that
Beverly made. Simple and elegant, it had four squares
on the front of a cube, each square a different color. It
held her smile.

Zip.

Hopefully these items would nourish me in the
Wild West.

CHAPTER 9

I didn't choose the University of California San Diego for the beach and the sun. But intuitively I knew that I needed to see the horizon. Having spent some of my childhood in Colorado, where one could see far and wide, I had learned to appreciate the openness of mind and spirit. During my junior high and high school years, the dense woods of New York felt claustrophobic and made me prone to melancholy. I believed that the western desert would be just the right antidote for my melancholic introspection.

Another reason for leaving New York was my absolute dedication to the study of science, a discipline that felt as inviting as the blue Pacific Ocean, teeming with possibility, promise and inspiration. When I had visited the university campus the year before, I knew that I wanted to be in this tidal pool of ideas. I was in heaven. I was about to embark on a wonderfully intellectual journey, a journey into nature.

On my flight west that fall, I took a weekend detour to Tulsa to see Nana and Ganco. I hadn't seen them for three years. My grandmother had been sounding strange on the phone, so I promised my mom I would check in on her.

My grandfather picked me up at the airport and drove me to their small duplex. A blast of cold air hit me as I entered the house.

"Agnes, we're home! I have Marney with me." His tone carried worry and concern.

My grandmother was watching her favorite soap opera. She turned her head to acknowledge my arrival, and immediately I could tell that something was very wrong. When she said my name, her speech was slow and slurred. Her eyes lacked their usual warmth. She turned her head back to the TV, passively watching the soap opera plot unfold.

I sat down next to her while my grandfather went into the kitchen. She didn't reach out to hold my hand like she used to. Her curly black hair hadn't been combed. Her body seemed to have given in to the weight of itself. She looked defeated and weak.

I found a brush in the antique-cluttered room and gently brushed her hair with the same love and care she used to give me. I could see her chest moving up and down, but her body sat there in total resignation.

The grandmother I knew was gone. The woman who had been so full of love, so full of spirit, had been gobbled up by something terrible.

I held her hand for hours. My grandfather shared his concerns and sorrow. He explained that the doctors were unable to diagnosis a specific illness.

That night, lying in bed, I thought of the human condition. Homo sapiens are part of nature and can decay quickly like a fallen tree. Nana had become a skeleton of herself. Her body was alive but her humanity was gone.

After a difficult weekend, I boarded a plane to San Diego. I tried to find comfort in the vast cloudscape outside the window. On my lap was Alice Walker's book, *In Search of Our Mothers' Gardens*. Her book was the last in my stack of summer feminist reads. I looked at it and wept.

My resolve to study biology deepened. My quest for knowledge about nature had become very personal. I felt that there must be a way to unlock the mysteries of human disease. Sitting in the plane flying over the Rocky Mountains, I reluctantly realized that I must include the mysteries of the human being in the realm of nature. I hadn't wanted to include homo sapiens, for I regarded nature as my escape from human darkness. But my love for Nana broke through this boundary. In that moment, I made a pact to myself to work to unravel the mysteries of the human condition within the context of nature. I owed it to my matriarchal lineage.

The University of California at San Diego was perched on a desert bluff looking down on the glistening Pacific Ocean. The natural beauty of the place was better than a strong cup of coffee for waking up the senses. The windswept canyons were teeming with life trying to survive the dry living conditions. I had never lived in an environment that held such promise and, at the same time, such bleakness.

The earth was so new here, having until recently been under the sea, that many of the creatures were still trying to find their niche. Cliffs hovering above the sea would daily succumb to the pressures of atmospheric life and return to the sea. These large exfoliations of the earth's skin left huge architectural canyons right on the sea's edge.

Black's Beach was directly down from the school and an easy walk from our dorms. Several of my friends were experts at California beach culture. Being an east coast girl, I was clueless.

Margaret would call me up and proclaim, "It's a beach day!"

The first time she invited me, I went into a frenzy. Surely this meant I needed to pack a lunch, get a sun umbrella, and find my bathing suit and my watch.

But when Margaret came to pick me up, she had nothing but a towel, a book, and that unmistakable bottle that smelled like coconuts. In fact, the sunscreen came through the door before she did.

"Let's go!" Margaret never needed a cup of coffee. She had grown up where the sun shines 345 days of the year and was "perky" by nature.

Once I had figured out that going to the beach was such a casual affair, Margaret and I spent most of our time there. She soaked up sun like it was food. One could almost see the rays being absorbed into her skin. She loved the sun, and it loved her. I liked to imagine that it loved her for her worship of it.

Because we were such dedicated students, we usually lugged our heavy textbooks along, convinced that we would actually read a chapter or two. Armed with my Vuarnets sunglasses from my trip to France, I would pledge to read 20 pages before putting my head down. Occasionally I succeeded, but usually the sound of the waves would cast a spell on me. The soothing, rhythmical sound took away all sense of time. Margaret seemed to have more perseverance than I, but even she would give in to the sounds of the great womb and fall into a deep sleep.

It was strange on these beach trips how the micro and the macrocosms were so interwoven. On the one hand, I had my book so I could ruminate on the minute details of photosynthesis. The text brilliantly outlined the complex dance of electrons through each molecule. Sometimes we took our little model kits down to the beach. They consisted of little colored balls and black sticks. The balls each represented an atom. For example, oxygen was always a red ball, carbon a black ball. The models always seem to have lots of red balls. The sticks represented the bonds between these atoms.

It was enormously fun to construct these conceptual aids. A molecule made no real sense to me, but the colored balls and the infrastructure did. I could see how the red balls always seem to attract the white or yellow balls. These models illustrated a gesture of contraction, moving inward.

But just as we were getting ourselves to think smaller and smaller, the grandness of the scene would sweep us up. There we were, pitched on this little spit of sand, lying fully exposed to the vastness of the great Pacific rim. Nature moved us from our books, to our imagination, to our dreams, to the archetypal rhythm of the great mother ocean. I would find myself staring at the waves for long stretches of time.

Although we weren't aware of it, we were dancing an unnamed but familiar dance of expansion and contraction. We were moving into the world of biology and then moving out into the grandeur of nature. This moving in and out had a profound effect on both of us. I felt so refreshed after "studying" on the beach. In some strange way it seemed more integrated in my mind when we studied at the threshold of the great abyss than in some cubicle in the library.

As I embarked on different studies that first year, the mysteries of nature began unfolding before me. I was being given the keys to understanding in areas as varied as muscle movement, inheritance of genetic traits, the chemical messengers of the brain, and the mathematical formula for the force of gravity.

A long road lay ahead, but I had the impression that the more profound human mysteries would be revealed to me over the next three years. The method was becoming clear. The professors were taking me on a journey that was reducing nature to her finest components. Contracting and distilling. The beach was for expansion and dilution. The end of the journey would reveal answers. I was sure of it.

CHAPTER 10

He strolled confidently into the lecture hall with wet hair and flip flops. The six-foot tall, broad-chested professor looked around at the three hundred students. I was sitting in the third row and could see the twinkle in his eyes as he began to talk.

"Good morning, everyone. Today we're going to be talking about the cell wall." Dr. Paul Saltman walked to the chalkboard with an athlete's grace. He was the kind of scientist I wanted to be. In the classroom he was a magician who took us on journeys to a world we couldn't see. Out of the classroom you could often find him surfing and playing like a dolphin in the grand Pacific. He was an explorer of life and wanted to share his playground with the world.

Week after week he showed us the beauty of the living cell. We learned about its architecture, the movement of nutrients, the transport of waste, and its replication of itself. Like Jules Verne, he opened up a world for me. Not one that was ten thousand leagues under the sea but one that was ten thousand times smaller than me.

After the lecture, I walked over to the Grove, a small café beneath a grove of large eucalyptus trees. I ordered a coffee with cream and a day-old bagel. I needed the caffeine, even though it pushed me over my budget for the week. I sat and waited for my friend Diane.

I listened to the blue green leaves swaying in the wind and pondered my mother's words from last night's phone call.

"Marn, the doctors in Oklahoma have diagnosed Nana with Lou Gehrig's Disease. It's a progressive neurological disease. She'll slowly loose her muscle function, especially the ability to swallow. My poor mother." She was crying by the end of the call.

As we talked, my own sadness had bubbled to the surface. I realize how much I had stuffed away my tears for my grandmother. It felt strange that there was nothing medically to do. But I knew what *I* had to do. Her diagnosis strengthened my conviction that I was here to learn and to contribute to the greater understanding of life and disease.

My nose caught the aroma of coffee, and Nana's face faded into my gray matter. I looked at the students sitting around the cafe. I was surrounded by a brainy buzz. I felt confident that this think tank by the sea would discover great things.

"Hey, Marn. Great goal last night!" Diane greeted me with a hug from behind.

I turned to see her Philadelphia-style smile and noticed her hockey stick in her hand. "Yeah, that was a fantastic pick you set for me. We make a good team," I said, as she walked around the table.

Diane slid into a chair and launched into a play-by-play recap of the game. I smiled and half listened as I took in her beautiful face. She had a scar over her left eye from a hockey injury. I loved her intensity and zest for life.

We studied neurology together, but we also played on the same indoor floor hockey team. Our co-ed team had three men and three women. My other friend Tawnya and I were the only novices. The others had all grown up on the ice in Canada or Philly.

We played on a basketball court with hockey goals set on each end of the playing field. Boards were placed in the four corners to make the game field an oval. These boards were also used for crushing the opponent while stealing the ball. Diane played center, I was left offensive wing, and Tawnya was the right offensive wing. Our trio was a powerhouse.

Diane, having played since she was nine, was the star of our trio. Her hockey stick became an extension of her arm. The three of us moved like ballet dancers as we did the setup, pass and score. This graceful floor dance was what brought the three of us together.

This semester I was on three intramural sports teams. It was perfect for getting the stress out of my body. Three nights out of five I had a game. Floor hockey was my favorite, but co-ed water polo with Margaret was a close second. We played in an indoor pool wearing inflated inner tubes. A common defensive move was to grab the edge of the inflated tube and try to overturn the opposite team. The previous week we had beaten the division III water polo team.

Margaret was a joy to play with. She competed like a playful sea otter who also happened to be the highest scorer on the team. I, on the other hand, wasn't a confident swimmer and was terrified of being dunked. But in the decisive game of the season, I paddled all the way from the defensive end, dodging defensive attacks, to position myself in front of the goal. I wound back my arm and proudly scored the winning goal. Margaret was so jazzed she bought tubs of ice cream and Oreo cookies for a victory party. We filled a bowl with ice cream, crushed cookies and ten spoons.

I looked at my watch and noticed a new set of students arriving at the Grove Cafe.

"Time for neurology lecture," I said, standing up and grabbing Diane's coffee mug.

We walked out of the shady grove and into the sharp springtime sun. The warmth soothed the top of my head. I liked how I felt in this climate. Back in New York the humidity had a way of dampening my thoughts. The desert air in San Diego made my mind feel clear and ready to absorb new ideas.

We waited at the door of the lecture hall to let our eyes adjust to the relative darkness inside, then found seats near the front. The journey began immediately as Professor Spitzer started to uncover the mysteries of a nerve cell and how it gets stimulated with shifts in sodium or potassium concentrations. As I listened, I marveled at the simple beauty of such a system. It became clear that the movement of these sodium and potassium ions was what moved my entire nervous system. The ions would create an action potential that would then stimulate the release of chemicals called neurotransmitters. This action must be altered in Nana somehow.

Spitzer was showing us a kind of map on an overhead projector. Like the New York City subway map, it was filled with detail and order. The constant movement of ions in and out of membranes looked like subway cars moving in and out of stations. It had a wonderful symmetry. The order that I saw in the waves on the beach or the budding of a flower was the same order I was learning here. Nature at her smallest level was mysterious but ordered and stunningly beautiful.

The lecture reminded me of my plots in the New York forest when I was a budding scientist. Now I was becoming a trained scientist. I was learning how to use my brain to understand nature's patterns. The weavings of life's truths were unfolding in front of me. Harmony, repetition, resonance, symmetry. The math of life.

"It's Mom. How was your day?" I heard my mother's soothing voice on the phone.

"It's been fantastic! Today I studied how the eye works. Mom, our eyes are really protrusions of our brain. The retina is so beautiful in its function. It can take light and convert it into chemicals that our body can understand. It has pigments within the cells that absorb the light."

"Pigments? Pigments like paint?" Beverly asked with laser-like attention.

"Gosh, yes. It must be true. Pigments absorb light and emit only a certain wavelength back. In the eyes the light is absorbed and then turned into a cascade of chemical events."

Gradually the discussion shifted from my latest discoveries to hers.

"I saw the most glorious colors today while I was teaching my students in SoHo. I took them to see the works of Susan Rothenberg. Marn, the blues in her works are wonderful."

When I left for school two years before, she began to take groups of women down to NYC and give guided lectures on the gallery scene in SoHo. The classes were well received. My mom was coming into a new phase as an artist. Now she wanted to share her knowledge.

We talked for an hour, discussing details. The world that I had been able to enjoy as a child was now being shard with others in our town. I was very proud of her.

*   *   *

Diane and I had passed all of our neurology exams so far. We had one final exam left. We started a two-day study marathon at the library at 6am. I found it easy to concentrate. The time whizzed by. King-sized hot tamales and Cracker Jacks helped when my blood sugar ran low.

I leaned back in my chair and rubbed my eyes. I was tired from reading but I felt very satisfied with the knowledge I had gained. I could spend my life learning about these beautiful mysteries of nature. For me they were tales of wonder that I was privileged to be learning about every week. Biologists already understand many of these mysteries, but what was the most exciting to me was the vast number that remained unsolved.

I left the exam feeling confident. This was a topic I really enjoyed, and I was sure I would pass the class. My confidence and enthusiasm paid off. After reading the posted test results, I walked back to my dorm, bursting with pride.

I knew that neurology was my muse.

CHAPTER 11

It was early morning when the phone rang in my new dorm room. I had decided for my third year to move back on campus. My sleeping roommate didn't stir as I lunged for the phone. Outside the window, the fog was moving quickly through the tall eucalyptus trees. *The fog won't burn off today*, I thought to myself.

"Hi, Marney. Your mother has something to tell you," said my dad in a serious, contracted voice.

I waited as he handed the phone to my mother.

"I've just been to the doctor's," Beverly said in a weak voice. "I have breast cancer." She explained that the prognosis was that she had a year or less to live. The cancer cells in her breast tissue were very aggressive. They had spread to her lymph nodes and were heading toward her bone marrow.

In a single day the entire course of our lives changed.

"Oh my god, Mom! How are you feeling? Do you want me to come home?"

"I have to go back for more tests later today. I'll be fine, honey. I want you to stay there and focus on your studies. It's so important. I'll be fine," she assured me, her voice switching to a stronger, motherly tone.

"Make sure you and Dad treat yourselves to a nice lunch and maybe a walk down to the pond. This is just preliminary information, Mom. We'll figure out how to deal with all of it later. Just make sure to take care of yourself."

"I will." she said.

Her voice had grown steadily stronger during the conversation. I could imagine her pulling deep inside herself, calling upon the Germanic DNA of her father and the levity of her French mother. The two qualities gave Beverly her beautiful strength and grace. She also had the love of her children, her husband, her mother and father, and her brother and sister-in-law to hold her up.

I sat on the edge of my roommate's bed and cried. I was scared. She had battled breast lumps for ten years. I realized now that there had been a constant hum of anxiety around her breast tissue. Now the imagined horror had become real. My roommate Angel, now fully awake, held me as I felt my world spinning out of control.

Despite my mom's struggles with depression, she always seemed so vibrant and alive. How could this be happening? How could nature strike down such a magnificent human being? She was in the prime of life.

I wiped away my tears and grabbed my toiletries for the shower. I stood under the warm stream, hoping the stimulation would keep the emotional numbness away. But I felt my mind churn slower and slower until it froze on a single thought: mortality. An inevitable but unexpected part of life.

The sun hurt my eyes as I walked to class. I wanted to hide in a deep, dark cave. The professor began his chemistry lecture by describing a process called entropy. I listened and took notes for a few minutes, but I couldn't stop myself from turning inward. I saw Beverly and, for the first time in my life, digested the horrific idea that my mother will die.

Who is Beverly? I muttered to myself. I had believed that she was a collection of atoms and molecules that joined together in such a way to make this unique person, but today that definition seemed insufficient. How could a collection of atoms make me feel so desperately sad? My mind drifted like a hot air balloon, carried on a strong current of memories.

My mother could wear her tailored Italian jacket with sophistication and grace, but she was never more than a step away from her southern farm roots. She had a lively way about her that reminded you of a sweet summer day. This spirit, combined with her attention to visual detail, made her a great story-teller.

The fodder for many hilarious tales was the ongoing drama between our resident squirrel and our ever persistent dog. At times she would take on the voice of both Malcolm the squirrel (of course the squirrel had a name) and Darwin the dog. Darwin was forever chasing Malcolm from below the phone lines while Malcolm would sit on the line and twitch his trail. This happened daily with the same outcome: the squirrel feeling like the victor and the dog feeling completely frustrated but determined. Like George Burns chasing behind Gracie's mistakes, this situation was always a source of laughter for our family.

Other stories would come from her childhood. I can still see Beverly and her brother Charles playing with the 15 calves my grandfather had purchased one summer. Her vivid descriptions would bring alive the smell of the calves, the heat of the Oklahoma sun, and the sheer joy of sharing an afternoon with such beautiful creatures. When she was animated, bluebirds seemed to sing around her head.

Walking back from class I remembered how, when I was younger, my father would get the red and black four-wheel-drive Jeep ready for a Saturday outing in the Rocky Mountains. Our family of four piled into it, and the Red Baron effortlessly ascended the steep dirt roads.

One day we drove to see the aspens in their quaking sea of gold. We were walking on a quiet dirt road, the fall colors all around us. The four of us laughed and played in the thin mountain air, each of us enjoying the pristine beauty. My father, brother and I all found it restful, while my mother was becoming part of the landscape, digesting every gold, blue and red.

When we returned home, she went to her studio and began to create the colors of the day. Not the exact colors but her internal mixing of them. Not the exact gold of the aspen, but her feeling of the aspen's gold through a new color.

The results were awesome. It's such a gift that artists have. And such a joy for the rest of us.

*   *   *

I woke from my daydreams to find myself walking toward the Grove Café to buy lunch. The lecture had barely registered. It didn't matter. I knew the path I was pursuing. The biologist's journey is to travel deeper and deeper into the heart of the matter. I was learning how to ask questions and, through experimentation, reduce natural processes down to the components that built the living being.

Cancer is from nature. It's a degenerative process that happens in cells. My intellect was seducing me into presuming that I could eventually understand nature, and, through my understanding, conquer cancer. This was the promise of modern science. The promise that there will be a cure.

I felt waves of sadness as I walked to the Central Library. I chose a desk in the stacks and surrounded myself with books about the cell. I sighed. The pain for my mother was immense. I knew there would be more to come. But I also knew that our collective understanding of this terrible disease was expanding day by day. Perhaps next year we would have a cure. I stared at the books around me. They seemed to give off an intense vibration. We've acquired a lot of knowledge, I assured myself. We must be close.

I knew that Beverly was in good hands in New York. I believed that she would be fine once they removed the cancer. She was a tough woman from Oklahoma. Her uncles rode in rodeos. Her grandfather was a Virginia coal miner. She came from very hardy stock. She would win this battle.

CHAPTER 12

The thick summer haze made it difficult to lift my bag from the carousel. The small duffle had seemed perfect when I packed it in the arid openness of California. Now, as I lifted it away from the big leather suitcases spinning round and round, I felt emotionally heavy and ill equipped for this visit. I had no idea what taking care of my mother would be like. She had completed her first round of chemotherapy while I was finishing my junior spring quarter. During this difficult time, we spoke weekly, sometimes daily. When the quarter ended, like millions of other devoted daughters, I came home to take care of my mother.

I spied my father as I moved through the baggage claim turnstile.

We walked slowly to the congested parking lot. I noticed that the usual confidence in his stride had been replaced by uncertainty. As he lifted my bag into the red Honda Civic I saw the fear in his eyes. I placed my hand on his shoulder and let the California sunshine radiate from my palm. It was dusk, and the streetlight left shadows on the parking attendant's face. I looked ahead onto the freeway and saw the muted purples and cobalt that come at the close of a day.

As we drove up the driveway to my childhood home, the house was dark except for the hallway light.

My mother had gone to bed. It was still early, but I felt tired, too. My father and I sat in the kitchen eating Georgia peaches that dripped onto paper towels. The house was very quiet.

"I'm glad you're here. It's been hard. Your brother has been doing poorly in school. Now he's out with his buddies all the time. Maybe in the fall he'll be able to refocus."

"The doctors are giving her a year." He paused to let me absorb this information. Then he added, "She's very excited you're here. She's struggling with her moods again. I think it's good you'll be here this summer to keep her company while I'm at work."

We finished our snack and walked upstairs to our bedrooms. I shut the door and fell into my old bed. The familiar loft and smell of the mattress relaxed my tense body. My room hadn't changed since I left three years ago. The old poster of Suzanne Farrell and Peter Martin still captured my attention with the dancers' simple beauty. My mind wandered back to my Sunday trips to NYC with my mother to watch the ballet at Lincoln Center.

I sat up, suddenly curious. I leaned over to open the drawer to my old school desk. Blues and reds popped out at me. I smiled, remembering my old track and field days. I picked up a ribbon, first place in the 100-meter dash. I thumbed through old letters stashed in the back cubby. I closed the desk and fell asleep. In my dreams I drifted from pleasant childhood memories to jolts of anxiety.

In the morning I sat across from Beverly at the kitchen table. She had made us the usual Red Zinger tea. I looked deeply into her eyes and thought about what the doctors had said. Only a year to live? I rolled this prediction around in mind, trying to grasp its meaning.

She had already endured massive amounts of radiation and chemotherapy to fight off this internal enemy. She had undergone a double mastectomy and had lost her hair. She had lost her appetite and her cheerful voice. I had been expecting to see terrible damage.

Yet she still looked radiant and beautiful. *Where are the signs of death?* I wondered. She was like a magnificent oak whose roots have been stricken by a terrible fungus. The tree would continue to grow big, heavy acorns even as she was dying deep within her core.

After tea I retreated upstairs to unpack my duffle. Soon I heard the sound of Mom's Dr. Scholls clogs making their way up the staircase. I listened until I heard her in her bedroom. I gathered myself to join her. It was time to hear the stories of the horrors she had endured.

She stood in a small hallway that housed my father's closet and hers. At the end of the hall was a long mirror. As I walked into this small hallway she turned toward me. She was naked. Her face was chiseled with anger.

"Look at the scars he left. I feel like I was just cut up. A complete butcher job!"

I could hardly look at her. I had seen her body many times and had marveled at its incredible beauty. Everything was in correct proportion. But I had not realized until this moment how beautiful her breasts had been. Now they were gone. Instead there was a wide slash of pink flesh on each side of her torso, the marks of the surgeon's work. Her small, concave chest looked as if it had been savagely attacked.

I had a flash of shared anger. Clearly the surgeon had removed her breasts with no regard for what they meant to her and her family. This tissue had nourished her children. It had given pleasure to her and her husband. Her breasts had been hacked down like redwoods in a forest.

"My back has been hurting me since they've been removed. I didn't realize how much counterweight my breasts created in the front. My entire posture has changed."

I gave her a tender hug. She felt so small, so vulnerable. I tried to give her some of my strength as I held her.

The first two days were quiet. On the third day my mother and I drove in the silver station wagon to a small health food store in Katonah. We needed supplies for home-made granola, a family tradition for many years. I threw a package of sesame seeds in the cart, while Beverly followed up with a package of coconut. We laughed at ourselves as we strolled through the tiny store.

Back at home we got out a huge baking pan and began to make the granola. I no longer needed the recipe; we had made this breakfast cereal hundreds of times. She pulled a huge wooden spoon from a ceramic vase and began to stir the toasted yummies. I kept her laughing with stories of my antics in San Diego.

When my mom took the last pan of granola out of the oven, I thought I caught a strange glimmer in her eye. It disturbed me, but I quickly dismissed it.

"Let's eat some now," I said.

"Great idea, Pips. Grab the raisins and I'll get the milk," my mother replied, using her favorite nickname for me.

I sighed with contentment as I took in all of the delicious, nutty flavors.

The next day the calm facade began to crumble.

I was walking down into the cold, moist basement to put laundry in the wash. In dark shadow under the copper pipes stood a stranger pouring turpentine into a mason jar. She was taking sips from the jar. She acted as if she didn't see me. I had trouble registering what was happening.

I suddenly moved into action, knowing that I was dealing with something terrible. I pulled the glass from her hand. I gasped when she glared at me with the same look I had caught a glimmer of yesterday at the oven. Grabbing her hand I pulled her up the stairs and made her wash out her mouth.

Beverly was gone. In her place was a frightening impostor. Her gestures were stunted and rough, not at all like her usual graceful motions. The color in her face had changed from a rosy glow to a sickly green. Her hair was tangled and knotted.

I put her in bed and stroked her head. As I pulled the sheets over her body a chemical smell filled my nostrils. She closed her eyes and fell into a deep sleep. The shock of what had happened began to settle on me like a heavy cloak. It didn't even occur to me to call for help.

Our family descended into a crazy maze. Nearly every day there was a bizarre, futile attempt at suicide. One afternoon she locked herself in the garage and left the old gray station wagon running with the side door wide open. My father found her sitting in the front seat waiting for him to come home from work.

Another time I heard a splash in the swimming pool while I was in the bathroom. I looked out the window and saw Beverly floating face down in the water. I ran like the wind down the stairs and jumped in the pool. As I pulled her from the water, I noticed ropes dangling from her arms and ankles. She had tied small rocks to the end of each rope. The rocks were so small that they almost floated in the water. She stared off into the distance as I removed the odd tangle of ropes and rocks.

I began to wonder if her obviously feeble suicide attempts were the only way she could express her anger and fear. Watching her express her internal suffering this way was unbearable. I became exhausted from weeks of constant monitoring.

One day that summer I was lying on my bed reading when she walked into the room.

"Marn, I'm going to drive to SUNY Purchase this morning to get some art supplies. I should be back for lunch."

"Are you feeling up to it?" I asked. I looked at her closely.

"Yes. I had a good night's sleep and I feel good," she replied convincingly.

"Have a good time." She had seemed very grounded and rational that day, so I felt confident, too.

But she didn't make it home for lunch. At three o'clock, she still hadn't returned. I was becoming seriously concerned and called my dad.

"Dad, Mom went out this morning and she's still not home."

"I'll leave work right now and we can go look for her."

When my father arrived we stood in the hallway for several minutes trying desperately to find clues to her whereabouts. We decided to start by calling the school, SUNY Purchase. Eventually we connected with the security department and told them our story.

I then started to call all of my mother's friends to see if they had seen her. She had a group of female artist friends that she was very close to. I had just hung up from one of the calls when the phone rang. It was a school security officer.

"Hello, Ms. Blair? We found your mother. It looks like she ate a giant bottle of Tylenol. But luckily she's alive."

"We'll be right there."

We arrived before the ambulance. Since her little red Honda was the only car in the vast school parking lot, the security officer hadn't had any trouble finding her. As my father and I approached the car I could see her collapsed with her head against the steering wheel. Her mouth was gaping open. Her breathing was shallow.

Time seemed to slow nearly to a stop as we waited for the ambulance to arrive.

At the hospital they determined that her liver was so toxic that she was just hours away from death. For the first week, she was so yellow that I thought I could smell a cloud of sulfur. Her entire body had an eerie yellow tinge.

This suicide attempt kept her in the hospital for two months. My brother, my father and I visited every day. I would sit by her bedside and stroke her hand. For the first week she was so weak that she didn't speak.

Then she appeared to gather her strength and slowly find her way back. A healthy skin color returned. The twinkle returned to her eyes. Most importantly she found her wonderful sense of humor again. Our family began to relax.

But I knew that her chances of overcoming cancer had become even slimmer. The mental instability that Beverly had struggled with when we were young had returned. Now she was fighting on two fronts. She was fighting the battle that was raging within her mind and the battle with the cancer that had invaded her body.

CHAPTER 13

A month after I returned from the devastating summer in New York, I opened the door of my dorm apartment. The familiar smells of Christina's rice cooking on the stove and Margaret's perfume soothed my nerves. I was entering my fourth year of studies. Margaret and I would take another year to complete all of the requirements to graduate with degrees in biology. Christina, on the other hand, was a more dedicated student and would graduate at the end of this school year.

I walked back to my bedroom to find Christina on the phone. We shared a west facing room. The late afternoon sun helped offset the hideous browns of the carpet, curtains and bed frames. I could tell that Christina was talking to her mother. Heavy tears fell from her chin to her lap but she kept her voice composed.

I sat quietly on my bed, eating a bowl of Christina's rice with soy sauce. I needed to study at my desk but wanted to be supportive of my friend. Our eyes met, hers shiny black from the tears, and I sent her a look of concern. I knew exactly what she was feeling.

This year Christina and I had developed a very close bond. Both of our mothers were diagnosed with breast cancer. Both of them had been given horrific prognoses. Although neither of us was accustomed to sharing our painful feelings, we often cried together. I admired Christina's determination to focus on her studies and found comfort in her strength.

We spent most of our days together in the library, sipping her wonderfully aromatic Chinese tea. This quarter I had classes in genetics, biochemistry, modern art, and quantum physics. We were taking physics together. I was managing to get good grades in all of my courses except physics. Often I would spend hours staring off into the library stacks, flashes of my mother's anguish making it impossible to focus on the pages of equations lying on the desk in front of me.

Christina hung up the phone. "It's so hard, Marn. She's in a lot of pain. But she said she's excited to meet you on spring break. Dad's going to make a big dinner like he always does."

"That sounds awesome. What does he cook?"

"Usually he makes his specialty dish, a whole fish cooked in black bean paste, and then a bunch of vegetable dishes."

"Thanks for inviting me. I'm really glad I'll get to meet your family."

*   *   *

Christina's large Chinese family lived in Palo Alto. Walking into her parent's modest home, I was immediately taken by the stillness. The front door opened into a formal living and dining room. The fireplace mantle was crammed with brightly painted ceramic figurines. Some had big Buddha bellies, and some had long flowing dresses and fans in their hands. Others were more mystical creatures. Their playfulness drew me in.

Christina's voice interrupted my contemplation. "Marn, come in the kitchen! I'm back here with my mom."

As I walked into the kitchen, I could see that this is where her family really lived. A welcoming beam of light filled the large space. Against the back wall was a bed where Christina was sitting, holding a woman's hand.

"Mom, this is Marney!" she declared enthusiastically.

Her mom sat up in bed. "Hello, Marney. Come in. Come in."

Christina jumped up from the bed and started to pour three cups of tea. Her mom adjusted the knit cap on her hairless head and slipped her feet into cozy slippers. She rose from the bed and started walking toward the back sliding glass door.

"Come see my birds!" she said with excitement.

The backyard was an apiary full of singing canaries of all different colors. Three huge cages were filled with the energetic birds. Her face sparkled as she introduced me to each one. I immediately loved this woman. Her zest for life reminded me of my mother.

As we stood laughing together in front of the last cage, Christina opened the sliding glass door. "Hey! The tea is ready."

I spent the rest of the afternoon in the warm, cozy kitchen drinking tea and eating snacks with Christina's mom. As the light began to fade, the kitchen began to bustle with dinner preparations. Her father, a dear man with a large, open, smiling face, started cutting vegetables with his two daughters. The feast was on.

Her mom had returned to her bed and lay there sleeping, a slight smile on her face. I sat on the edge, chatting with Christina as she chopped green onions.

Soon the kitchen became a whirlwind of aromas and chattering relatives. At least ten family members had joined the celebration, all of them speaking Mandarin and bustling around, placing platters of food on the large, extended table. I got up to help Christina place plates and cups on the table. It was filling so fast with sumptuous food that I had to move dishes aside to find space for the plates. In the middle of the table was a huge lazy susan with soy sauce and many spicy condiments.

We all sat at the glorious table and spent hours enjoying the food and each other's company. Finally I gestured to Christina to follow me to the quiet living room. I was exhausted.

"Had enough, Marn?" Christina chuckled.

"Oh, my god. I can't eat another bite. But your grandma just keeps heaping the rice on my plate."

"Well, you should learn some Mandarin then," Christina teased. She led me to her bedroom. "Here, rest in my room."

I closed the door behind me and gave a sigh of relief. I wondered how they had the stamina to keep going. I closed my eyes and drifted off.

A roar of laughter from the kitchen woke me from my nap. I looked at the alarm clock by Christina's bed and sat up with a jolt. I had been sleeping for four hours. I combed my hair with my hands and walked into the kitchen.

It was a beehive of activity. Seven adults were engrossed in a game of mahjongg. The room was filled with the noises of clanking tiles and tea cups, teasing and laughter. In the midst of the clamor, Christina's mom slept happily on her single bed, dreaming of her birds and her happy family.

*   *   *

My mother seemed to stabilize that summer as the days grew shorter and the crisp air began to drift down from Canada. It felt like a vice grip had been released. She began to focus on her cancer treatments and enrolled in an experimental drug trial using a new drug called Tamoxifen at Mount Sinai in New York City.

I had received a D in physics in my last quarter. It was the first time in my life I had earned such a miserable grade. I could feel something brewing inside me. After nearly four years of biology, I didn't feel any closer to helping my mother or understanding nature. Instead

I began to develop a suspicion that both nature and the human mind were unpredictable, chaotic, and lethal.

For my last two quarters I had taken neurology classes so that I could focus on understanding the brain. I found them intellectually exciting. They opened up an entire new area of questions, and I was beginning to see that the brain was made of layers and layers of neural chemical processes. But what was the mind?

That summer I found an exciting internship with Doctor Robert Livingston. I signed up without hesitation. The project was digitizing and mapping the brain of a chimpanzee.

"The pain reflex is very complex, and after thirty years of study we still do not fully understand the entire mechanism," Dr. Livingston quietly told us interns on the first day. He looked like a whimsical Don Quixote, but his work was anything but whimsical. He had won a Nobel Peace Prize several years before I began working for him. I didn't know this about him at the time; he was too modest to mention it.

I worked long hours in his office overlooking the Pacific Ocean. At lunch I would grab my paper sack and sit on the beach watching other students surf. The soothing sound of the ocean cleared my brain of the whirling curiosities I had accumulated during the morning hours.

Each day another intern and I would scan slices of a monkey's brain into a data base. The tissue on each slide seemed so delicate and incapable of holding memories, emotions and pain. I stared at the intricate, swirling patterns of neural processing and wondered how they could cause such complex emotions as anguish and elation.

The goal of the project was to create the first ever 3-D image of a monkey brain. Livingston hoped that the completed image would further our understanding of the structure which, in turn, would give us insight into the function of the various parts of the human brain. Structure follows function.

The monkey's brain was clearly much more than a mass of cauliflower-like tissue. There were distinct structures that looked very different from one another. I was especially interested in the limbic center, a part of the brain that lies in the interior of each hemisphere and is responsible for emotional processes. This beautiful structure, thought to be old cortical tissue, is in the shape of a horn. Within the heart of the limbic system is the hippocampus. This is where memories are stored. The entire limbic system works together to process and store emotional life, in this case the emotional life of a monkey.

The hypothalamus is richly connected to the limbic system via neurons. It is through these neural pathways that mind and body are connected. This part of the brain acts like a switch. It is an extremely influential structure that converts neural impulses into endocrine responses via the pituitary. The hormones that arise from the pituitary affect how our bodies react. For example, the impulse to run after being scared comes from these sets of pathways. Fear can drive this entire system. Prolonged fear can suppress the immune system.

Even in this monkey brain tissue I could see these structures. This monkey, like me, received impulses from the brain stem and from its higher brain, the cerebral cortex. It was extremely humbling to witness these structural similarities.

Just as fascinating as the brain tissue was the man behind the project. Dr. Livingston had an incredible office with large windows overlooking the Pacific and a door that was always left ajar for young interns like me. Like a moth drawn to a glowing street lamp, I would walk into his office, seeking his calm voice. We had many interesting chats there. Most of our conversations had nothing to do with neurology. I was continually amazed at this elegant man's warmth and openness.

Most mornings Dr. Livingston talked on the phone while I entered data in the room next to him. I would pause in my work so I could listen to every word of his upbeat philosophical discussions.

One morning when I was preparing slides for the microscope, I was finding it hard to concentrate. The crisp light from the ocean teased my attention away from worlds that were too tiny for my naked eye. I went into Dr. Livingston's office and sat down in one of his brown leather chairs. He was writing, and I waited quietly for his attention.

"Hello, Marney, dear," he sang out. "How is your day progressing?"

"Great. I had a couple of questions about the data we entered yesterday and..."

"Oh, yes, we can get to that, but I just had the most wonderful conversation with my dear friend in India, the Dalai Lama. We're working on this project together and I'm going to meet him in Amsterdam soon."

I had no idea who the Dalai Lama was. As he continued to talk, I was distracted by the way the morning sunlight bounced off the white paper on his desk and illuminated his generous face. It appeared that the warmth of the sun was merging with the warm joy in his face. I watched in astonishment.

This man, a prominent scientist, was connected to the world in a way that I knew nothing about. I was witnessing a lightness to his being that I had never seen before. My eyes had been focused on tissues and structures all morning; now they were seeing something mysterious that had nothing to do with a science lab.

I told myself that I needed to get back to my work. I would remember this moment and deal with it later. I left his office, the wonderful aura that surrounded Dr. Livingston continuing to blanket me. I smiled at the feeling and felt blessed to be working with him.

What I didn't know at the time was that another important door was opening for me. A door to the world of eastern philosophy.

CHAPTER 14

One winter afternoon as I was studying in my dorm room at UCSD, I felt a jolt of panic. It was the second year of Mom's battle with breast cancer, and the thought suddenly hit me: *my mother is dying a slow and horrifying death.* Her body was desperately fighting the voraciously multiplying cancer cells. Her mind was fighting the demons of anger and fear.

I couldn't make sense of the brutality. A lioness hunting a gazelle is a kind of brutality, but the hunt only lasts a short time. The gazelle isn't tortured for years. My mother's kind of suffering was unnatural.

Hoping to curb the panic, I stepped outside into a warm ocean breeze. The salty mist slowly calmed me. I walked toward a grove of eucalyptus trees that I had spied earlier that morning near the lecture hall. I stretched my body out on the grass and felt the earth beneath me. I closed my eyes and imagined ion channels and mitochondria, suicide attempts and dividing cells.

After a few minutes, I opened my eyes and checked my watch. Grateful that I still had a half hour until embryology lab, I closed my eyes again and reviewed mental pictures of the cell. It was a world that we would never truly know. Even when we peer into a microscope, our brains superimpose stored images upon the light our eye receives. We never see without inter-pretation.

Later in the embryology lab I did as our profes-sor instructed and filled a needle with 10cc of nicotine and injected it into the fertilized chicken ovum. My fif-teen classmates and I all hunched over our microscopes, plugged into the tiny world before our eyes. A beautiful ball of cells shimmered in the electric light. The cell mass was giving off its own light. As the minutes passed, we watched the blastula turn in space while producing a new set of cells. This tiny life-becoming was changing and growing at its own rate, scripted by the DNA inside each cell.

Hearing my classmates' murmurs of excitement, a wave of guilt passed over me. I didn't like being a voyeur, or worse still, a Dr. Frankenstein. Why do we humans give ourselves the power to harm for the sake of our curious minds? I pushed my feelings aside, as I had learned to do. I needed to concentrate. A scientist must remain objective, and I also needed to get a good grade in this class.

The entire lab was the size of three garages. Everything was new for this promising generation of scientists, from the brown wood and black slate benches to the silver faucets and gas spigots. We were expected to bring humanity into the new era of modern molecular science.

The professor had set up an elaborate experi-ment. Over the course of ten weeks we would study the effects of nicotine, caffeine, and alcohol on fertilized chicken eggs, frog eggs and fish eggs. Left alone these eggs would have had the opportunity to grow into hatchlings. In *our* hands, however, the outcome would be manipulated to satisfy our curiosity.

The following week I took my nicotine-inoculated eggs out of the incubator and carefully placed them on my lab bench. I had anticipated some odd results, but what I found left me staring in horror. The young lives had been altered by the chemicals to another expression of themselves. Some of the embryos had divided into two spheres, demonstrating that they would create two chicks joined at the middle. Other embryos were developing larger than normal head regions. These mathematically inspired precision fractals were creating creatures of bizarre distortions. I shook my head, and the scientist in me let the feeling of horror travel out the door.

I began to draw in my lab notebook exactly what I saw. I was still learning to be objective, to remain detached. After an hour I had two pages of sketches. Two days later I would repeat the process in order to document the further changes these chemicals were creating. This exercise gave me a strange relief and a way to preoccupy my thoughts. I was training myself to record only what I could clearly document.

These exercises also set in motion a response to pain that would take me a decade to unravel. At the time I wasn't aware of how I was becoming conditioned to segregating my emotions, stuffing them in a box somewhere in the depths of my brain. On a primal level, I knew what I was doing was unnatural, even grotesque. But the perversion of needing to know why reinforced my behavior of burying my feelings.

Four years into my studies I began to long for the days when I walked in the woods with my dog. Those meandering hikes were becoming a faint memory, overshadowed by the construction of this house of Biological Knowledge. In the scientist's pursuit to understand life, nature can be made ugly. As ugly as the scars on my mother's chest.

I tried to treat nature as something that could be predicted through mechanical means. Molecules worked like a watch, minds worked like computers, and flocks of birds worked like robots flying the same course every year because this is what they were programmed to do.

Somewhere deep within this maze of intellectual curiosity, I was losing the freedom that I felt in the dark, moist woods. Yet I continued to be seduced by my greedy, curious intellect. It gave me hope that I could control the outcome of life. All I needed to do was work harder at understanding the molecules responsible for my mother's cyclical depressions and for my grandmother's inability to control her muscular function.

My desire to solve the mystery of my matriarchs overshadowed everything. Both my grandmother and mother had demonstrated to me that the molecules in our minds can be dangerous. I needed to find the mechanisms that controlled those molecules. If I could understand this mind machine, I would be able to save them from their suffering.

The race was on, and I wasn't sure how much time I had.

That evening after embryology lab, the phone rang in my dorm room. It was my weekly call from my mother.

"I wanted to reach you before you went off to dinner. How was your day?"

I gave her a brief recap and then asked what she was doing.

"I was just sitting here in the kitchen watching the fish tank." My mother's voice was strong and clear.

"Yeah? What're the fish doing today?"

As she started to answer, I only half listened as I made a quick assessment. *She sounds good. Perhaps she's feeling stronger. Maybe her mental state is more stable.*

"I had to take that ornery fish out of the tank again. He's been chasing all of the other fish all morning. So I put that stinker in a jar. I'm giving him a time out. I watched him while I was eating lunch. He seemed to calm down after his break so I put him back in the tank. Hopefully he'll behave himself."

We both laughed. I gazed out the window at the gentle wind stirring the eucalyptus trees. I could feel this precious mother/daughter moment sealing itself in the caverns of my brain. The sound of her voice, the timing of her stories, made my muscles and stomach relax.

The calm didn't last. As we continued to talk, pain slowly slipped into my feet, worked its way up to my lower back, and lodged behind my eyes. It was so dense that I felt that if I tried to look at it, it would slice my head open. Unconsciously I decided to ignore this villain until I could muster all of my strength to fight him.

"How are you feeling this week, Mom?"

"I still don't have an appetite, but I'm trying to eat as much as I can. But I'm feeling good. I've been sleeping, and I'm not feeling crazy. I miss you and your brother." Having finished her weekly status report, she went on to describe a new project she was working on.

"I have an idea to film the art in SoHo galleries and describe the work. It'll be like a magazine article, only in video format. I'm going to call it Art 21."

I could hear her excitement and thought to myself, *You can't keep a good woman down!*

"I'm in the process of getting permission from gallery owners and have interviews with some galleries tomorrow. And I got to talk with the Mary Boone gallery! They're featuring David Salle's work. They're letting me put his work in my video."

"Mom, this is fantastic! What an incredible idea! Has anyone ever done this before?"

"No, and I'm really excited about it. I'm also working with a director called Juan Downey. He's incredible. I write the text, and he brings in the crew to film in the galleries."

We talked for almost an hour about art and her vision for the future of modern art. She wanted to use her knowledge to make modern art accessible to everyone. She was riding the magic carpet of her muse. This project had the potential to be big, really big.

Big enough, perhaps, to distract her from the constant medical interventions. Her vulnerable forty-five-year-old body was enduring physical torture. Torture that was keeping her alive. Like a boxer knocked down in the ring, she would grab the ropes again and again to pull herself back into life. She needed to give back to the world. My mother was driven to create and share with others.

CHAPTER 15

I was living with Margaret in a condo in the town of Del Mar, just north of San Diego. She was in the process of applying to medical schools. Christina had graduated and was now living in Palo Alto to help take care of her dying mother. My own mother was in her fourth year of cancer treatments. Our family had reached a strange plateau, our bodies and minds numb from the stress yet still hoping that she might overcome the cancer.

Margaret and I spent most of our free time together, often hiking in the desert, driving to Baja for lobster and margaritas, or just hanging out near the beach with her sister Kay. I was starting my fifth year of college. I was studying hard, playing hard, and eating buckets of antacids.

I liked the condo development where we lived because of the barren roads behind us. They were perfect for running. In the early morning hours I could see bobcats coming home to their dens. Margaret liked the gym and Olympic-size swimming pool. She swam a mile every morning.

The sun was breaking the horizon as I drew in a deep breath. I was enjoying a long run among the manzanita. Jack rabbits darted in and out of the low, dense scrub. I could afford a two-hour run since I was at the beginning of my spring break.

As I walked into the apartment I saw the light flashing on our answering machine. I punched the button and went into the kitchen to pour myself a large glass of orange juice. My nerves jumped. It was my dad's voice. I walked over to the machine and pressed rewind.

"Marn, I need you to call. Your mother isn't doing well. I had to admit her to a mental hospital. She's at Silver Hills. I think you best come home for a while. Her physical health is deteriorating. Call me."

I crumpled into a chair and stared off into space, imagining the horrible state of mind my mother must be in again. I stood up and dialed home. In a tired voice my father explained how he had committed my mother once again to a mental hospital. This was her third time. I felt a strange sense of relief when I hung up the phone. *She is alive and she is safe.*

I arrived home to a sad, still house. It was tidy and the dishes were done. Actually it was *too* tidy. As I would soon learn, it was because he wasn't really living in it. Every night he would grab a quick meal, then rush over to the hospital to visit my mom.

I felt the sticky air on my arm as we drove toward Silver Hills. I took in the grand old maples on the drive. Their dark bark gave me comfort. I wanted to hold on tightly to the essence of the black bark. It was a good black.

We parked the car and walked into the lobby. Bold blues, reds and yellows jumped out at us. The light was falsely cheery and too bright. I could feel the comfortable black light of the maples dissipate inside me.

My mom reflected that same false light as she walked cautiously into the room. It hurt my eyes, and I tried to deflect it to see the real Beverly light. But it wasn't there.

It was heartbreaking to watch my parents embrace in this loony bin. I could tell that for her it was just an act. She seemed to be barely holding on to reality. I longed for my real mother. *Where had she gone? Why did her face look as if she were wearing a mask? Was my real mother behind there trying to free herself from this impostor?*

During our visits patients would pace up and down the hallways making various animal noises while my mom would cling to her thin thread of sanity. Trying to demonstrate that she was doing better, she would ask how my studies were going or how my father's work day had gone.

My dad could endure the torture for about an hour. Then he would stand abruptly and give Beverly a hug. We'd walk her back to her brightly colored bedroom. Her body would relax, and she'd gaze at us with relief to be back in seclusion. I'd kiss her goodnight and squeeze her hands tightly.

Outside in the Connecticut summer air after one of our visits, I could hear the crickets call. We rolled down the car windows and drove past the hospital's manicured lawns. Dad looked over at me sadly and our eyes locked. His hand moved to the stereo and pushed in the cassette tape.

It was the Grateful Dead. We sang at the top of our lungs to the majestic oaks streaming by. "Sugar magnolia, blossoms blooming, heads are heavy and I don't care, saw my baby down by the river...." Jerry Garcia's voice could always clean the wounds.

Later in the week, the unthinkable occurred.

My uncle Charles called and sadly reported that my grandmother had passed away. Nana and Ganco had been living with my uncle's family in Austin, Texas. I was surprised at the news. I had been so preoccupied with the family chaos that I didn't know that my grandmother was so close to dying. Uncle Charles and I talked on the phone for over an hour. I told him that it was unlikely that Mom would be able to attend the funeral.

"Uncle Charles, I can have my father ask the doctor if she can leave. But she may not feel like she can make the journey. I'm so sad and sorry. Did Nana die peacefully?"

"She was very comfortable when she died. She had a twinkle in her eyes until the very end. Dad was wonderful, too, taking care of her all these years."

"Good. Thanks for the call. I love you, Uncle Charles. I'll try to come this weekend for the funeral."

My father and I drove to the hospital to tell my dying mother that her mother had died. This time we didn't listen to the Grateful Dead. We rode in silence.

"What? You want to go to the funeral?" my dad asked Mom, his voice heavy with worry. "Everyone will understand if you can't make it."

"No, Bill, I'll be fine. I want to go. Really. I'll be fine. Marney can come with me. Everything will be fine. I'm feeling better these days," she answered, her voice unusually calm.

My father and I looked at each other, silently asking ourselves how we could deny her this wish.

"If the doctor gives you the go-ahead, then I'll buy the plane tickets," my dad announced.

I was in anguish. I knew that the trip would turn into a nightmare if my mom suddenly had an episode of craziness. But I wanted to attend the funeral myself and be with my aunt and uncle. I also wanted my mom to be able to pay her respects. I decided that I would travel with my mom if she got permission to go.

The next day I watched her gather a few of her things for the trip to Texas. My mother had a love-hate relationship with this hospital. She told me that being confined made her feel safe from herself. But she also got enraged at the injustice of having to spend the last days of her life in this confinement. As she packed up her toothbrush and hair brush I could see that she was excited to have a break from the hospital.

I didn't realize that in her mind it was a permanent break.

When we got home I walked upstairs with her to pack her suitcase. I pulled it out of the closet and set in on her bed. She pushed it to the floor and climbed into bed.

"Mom, what on earth are you doing?"

"I'm not going to Texas. I'm staying right here."

Terror and disgust washed over me. I had been tricked. As I watched her pulling the comforter up to her neck, I took in the deep tragedy I was living at this moment. My mother had used her mother's funeral as an excuse to escape from the mental hospital. I sank back against the wall and slid to the floor. I watched her chiseled face. Her eyes shot out darts of cold blue light that traveled around the room. The crazy woman that she had hidden so well in the hospital was emerging before my eyes. She became a different person. The way her lips were shaped, the way she held her hands, her entire posture as she lay in bed had changed.

Beverly stiffened her body like a child in a tantrum. She became a being that could only think and act toward one goal, how to remain in this bedroom. My dear mother, who in sane moments loved her own mother, was now incapable of love. Instead she had become capable of extreme manipulation and deep deception. She was fighting for survival at any cost.

I walked down to the kitchen and sat staring at a Georgia O'Keeffe painting of her first airplane ride. The painting is blue with a series of white clouds dotting the canvas. My eyes moved beyond the horizon she had painted, and I rested my mind there, finding freedom in the expansive light. I was trying to lose the image of my mother's steely cold face in the endless blue horizon.

I finally allowed my tears for my grandmother to fall. I had been holding my sorrow for her in a very small drawer near my heart. I kept the rest of my heart boarded up against the eventual hurricane that would rush in when my mother died. The small drawer was for all of the other feelings. I opened it and could remember the smell of Nana's perfume. I could see her beautifully round, open face. Big, heavy tears rolled down my cheek. As I wiped them away, I realized that I needed to shut the drawer so that other sorrows couldn't escape.

I wouldn't be going to my grandmother's funeral. I needed to focus on my mother. And right now, my father and I needed to accomplish what felt like an impossible task: forcing my mother to return to the place she hated. For nearly an hour we struggled to get her down the stairs and into the car, her arms and legs flailing. Finally she was exhausted enough that we managed to get her safely inside.

As my father and I drove her back to the hospital, I struggled with my feelings of contempt. I had never felt this way about my mother before, but the combination of physical struggle, emotional games, and the missed funeral had put me over the edge.

Her psychiatrist was waiting for her when we arrived. The attendants put her in a wheelchair, and she disappeared out of sight.

My father and I drove home, Jerry Garcia singing in the background. I didn't bother to listen. Instead I was searching my heart for compassion for my mother.

I watched the stately maples go by and wondered about the human condition. *Are humans really part of nature? Where is the tragic, chronic suffering in nature? What is the evolutionary value of such suffering? Why does such suffering seem to be unique to the human condition?*

CHAPTER 16

Graduation brought me to another crossroads. I had my diploma announcing that I was ready to begin my life as a scientist, but this world of reasoning didn't explain what I was living through. Neurology cannot fully explain the diseased human mind. Physiology cannot explain the languishing in pain. In all my years of schooling, no one ever touched on the topic of dying. Although a certainty of life, death was avoided.

Fortunately, my dad had us all focus on lighter concerns that winter. He came up with a brilliant idea, a big mobile home of an idea. He called it "Club Fred," a take-off on Club Med and the Chevy Chase movie "Vacation."

RV's to me were perfect symbols of the 1980s California lifestyle. I don't know how conscious it was on my father's part, but that summer he rented a big, ugly, brown RV and set out to immerse himself and my mother in the culture that his two children had chosen.

"Here's our RV uniform," my dad announced, holding out a bag. I opened it to find four red baseball hats. They had "Club Fred" emblazoned on the front. I put one on. It felt perfect.

Club Fred was going to take us from San Diego to Northern California. My brother was a new student at UC Santa Cruz. Since my brother and I were both becoming Californians, my parents wanted to connect to our new lives. And we all wanted to create new ways to relate to each other, away from the horrors of our family life in New York.

We all began to relax as our Club Fred moved north. We soon left behind the southern warmth and moved into the cold dampness of northern California. My mother was fairly sane as we wound through oak groves, green grasslands, and finally the giant redwoods. Despite our calm, however, there was always the "elephant" in the RV: the unspoken anxiety about her physical and mental health.

We crossed Marin county and drove north on 101 into Sonoma. The golden light had a soothing effect. It felt warm and cozy even when the fog would weave in and out of the 300-foot redwoods. We made a stop when we saw an enticing sign for the Hacienda Winery. Good local wine was the medicine we all needed.

The winery sat in a natural meadow. Among the grapevines were lush wild grasses and shrubs. In true Sonoma fashion, the winery had no pretensions. Wine was just a small player in the glorious nature around us.

We walked the grounds and eventually bought a bottle of sweet wine to go with our lunch. The setting and food were simple. We had a loaf of sour dough left over from San Francisco, a wedge of Sonoma jack, dry salami, and my dad's favorite snack, potato chips. As we sipped the wine, I marveled at how a twisted vine could pull the humble sweetness of this land into such juicy fruit.

As if the wine were a magic potion, the family atmosphere shifted that day among the ancient red giants. We laughed as we had long ago, drinking our fill of life's exquisite beauty as it wrapped around us like a golden blanket.

After lunch we played among the old companions, my mother and I darting like witches in and out of the giant trunks. She wore my brother's poncho and I an old wool sweater knitted by my Norwegian friend. Beverly was relaxed and full of life within this natural cathedral. She gazed out from inside a large trunk, the redwood's timeless beauty framing her lovely face.

The soft light drifted through the misty air. In this grand presentation of nature, our lives seemed perfectly placed. There was no sadness, no regrets. We just *were*. It was easy to be and to be with each other. The soil, wind, water, and light weaved around and through us, filling our heads with ancient melodies.

I desperately wanted to stay here, among our giant friends, until my mother's body decided to expire. The woods would take in the fear. The woods would absorb our pain. These grand trees could buffer anything.

Slowly we all emerged from our seduction. We reluctantly walked out of the redwoods to our house on wheels. It was getting late in the day. I held my mother's hand as my brother drove the RV toward the Mendocino coast. I could feel the loving life force that I knew so well. I thought of her as the child who grew into a beautiful woman who carried two children in her womb. She tended to these children, her husband and others that she loved. She was unique, like all of us. A unique human being and a blessing to all of us who loved her.

My brother followed the signs to Fort Bragg. The road to the coast was narrow and twisted in and out of damp redwood groves. Alongside I could see a river moving with us toward the open Pacific.

We stopped for the night at Van Damme State Park. My father and I decided to hike on a narrow path near our campsite, while my brother and mother opted to stay inside the cozy RV for a nap. The trail meandered through scrubby, aromatic plants that had been gnarled and sculpted by the constant wind. Despite the hard conditions, they gifted the dunes with brilliant yellows, reds, and blues. The colors lifted the damp, redwood haze from my head. Eventually the trail opened to a sandy bluff overlooking the ocean.

I stood and looked out over the great Pacific. My father joined me.

"Marney, what is that?" he suddenly gasped. "Can you see that spout far off in the distance?"

"Oh wow, dad, it's the great whales migrating!"

We stood silently, watching keenly for the next spout of water. My father began to cry. It was a cathartic, slow weeping. I didn't say a word. I knew that he was overtaken by the same feelings I was experiencing. Awe at the enormous, simple beauty of it all. A feeling of primal connection with this magnificent mammal that was so far away but so near in our hearts. But the salt on his face was also there for Beverly. His wife, his lover and simply his dear Beverly.

We stood there for a long time, staring off to a point on the horizon. The ocean was a brilliant, crisp Pacific blue. Slowly, like the waves that were moving in, the crisp color was dissipating. The water took on the blue-gray of a cloudy day. Then it faded into gray. The fog had moved in.

"We'll be lucky if your mom lives six months," my father said out of the blue, as he turned to walk back to the RV parking lot.

Having nothing to add, I walked silently next to him.

CHAPTER 17

Later that summer I returned to New York to help my father and brother care for my mother. My mother could maintain her sanity during the cool months, but life always unraveled after the summer solstice. The great pausing of the sun when it reaches its apex invariably triggered an intense manic episode. It was as if the solar fire radiated down into her heart and blood, and the heat could only escape in a form of exaggerated excitement.

The cancer was aggressively moving from her breast to her lymph nodes, to her liver and bloodstream. About every six months, the doctors would give her a prognosis of death. Beverly defied every prediction. She was now in her sixth year of cancer.

Countless times she would say to my father as he sat by her bedside in the medical hospital, "Back to par tomorrow, Bill." With that, despite the nurses and doctors warning us that she wouldn't make it to dawn, she would be back in the morning with a sparkle in her eyes.

These miraculous recoveries were uplifting for all of us. Her body would gain vitality and her mind would be restored. But as the years progressed, the combination of her cancer and manic moods became more and more toxic. They seemed to feed off each other. As the cancer weakened her, her mind fought ferociously to survive.

At first her elevated moods were exciting to be around. Then they became exhausting and finally maddening. She never stopped. She wasn't satisfied with any activity she was doing. She slept and ate very little. She would sit for five minutes then want to get up and walk around. I would read to her for two minutes, and then she would want to walk around the kitchen. No one in the family could keep up with her, so we opted to take shifts. This arrangement seemed immensely better than sending her off to yet another damn hospital.

"Marn, play that record again," Beverley whispered with great effort.

She was lying in the living room, barely alive. But, as usual, she wasn't resting. I couldn't understand it. She was dying, yet she seemed to have endless energy.

Seeking a moment of relief, I gazed out the window. The summer sun was tempered by the large maple leaves outside the window. *What a beautiful day it is,* I thought to myself. The natural world seemed uncomplicated, peaceful. I turned my attention back to my mother.

"You want to hear Kathleen Battle again?" I was getting exasperated. I had been on watch since 4 am, and now it was twelve hours later. She was terrified to be alone. The company of her family proved to her that she was still alive.

I put the album on and sank into the leather sling chair. She was lying on the gray felt couch, a favorite resting place for the whole family. I could imagine the delicate gray threads wrapping around her and soothing her vulnerable body.

She began to doze off, and I tried to ease her into a peaceful sleep with my own breathing. I willed her to reach that restorative state, but just as her body began to relax she sat straight up in a panic.

"I do not want to die!" she yelled out, her eyes glassy with fear.

"Mom, you're not dead. You're here with me. See, you're here with me. I can put that music on again for you. Would you like that?"

She didn't answer. She was consumed with the agony of her mortality. I held her and rocked her in my arms, my tears moistening her flannel shirt. When she began to calm down, I turned the music on for about the tenth time in the past twelve hours. Kathleen Battle's voice filled the room with honey sweet tones. Her voice, as she sang classical ballads, was truly magical.

I watched the fear dissolve from my mother's exhausted body. I wondered about the quality of her life. Perhaps she could feel, as she laid her tired head down, the years of family daydreams woven into the gray felt of the couch. Perhaps she could feel the primal beauty in a voice like Kathleen's. I let the tears fall, knowing that they were for my longing and desperation at losing the source of my life, my mother.

As the light dimmed in the house my mother would move to the guest room on the first floor. It was an awkward room, filled with two large mahogany beds and antiques from my mother's childhood. The dark mahogany stain matched the dark colored rug on the floor. I avoided this room throughout my childhood. It felt so old and dark compared to the modernist-minimalist style of the rest of the house.

The old beds where my mom languished night after night had belonged to her aunt Pauline, her mother's sister. This aunt, unable to bear her own children, adored my mother and affectionately called her "Day-Day." I can still hear my mother's bright "Hello, Pauline" as she answered the phone. They had a strong connection throughout my childhood.

Night after night, day after day, we attended to my mother, the desperation in her behavior creating a bizarre reality for the entire family. We were all living in dream time, trying to weather the storms of a woman furious about dying. We witnessed the horrid fact of life: Death gets to choose when. Death gets to choose how. Death gets to choose why.

But death was not the victor that summer. Beverly slowly regained her strength. And I, unknowingly, continued to grow the armor that had already allowed me to endure years of shock and that would allow me to endure much more.

CHAPTER 18

In the photograph taken at Oklahoma State University in 1961, Beverly sits proudly with her peers, looking directly into the camera as she waits for the moment to be recorded. The pencil drawing she holds has won first prize. This was the first official confirmation of what she knew from an early age: she was an artist.

She had already found her home, the place where she felt most understood and accomplished. The world of line and shadow, form and color had become her lifelong companion.

She went on to further her understanding of the creative world by working toward an MFA at the University of Colorado in Boulder. There she developed a unique sense of color and style. She found her own voice. This voice spoke of colors building upon each other to create a portal to an emotional experience. Each color she mixed had her signature of personal discovery. Each painting was a small opening into the light of her soul. Over and over again she made herself vulnerable to the world. She wanted the world to witness the beauty that she sensed.

During the years I spent understanding the mechanics of the biological world, my mother dramatically changed the course of her art. For decades she had worked with oils on canvas or water color on paper in abstract expression. In the late 80s she began to move the colors and their emotional footprints into three-dimensional forms. Her paper twisted and turned off the wall and into the room. Her work grew larger and larger, reaching five feet in length and projecting up to two feet off the wall. Each piece was a voluptuous celebration of life.

Even when breast cancer struck, her drive to perfect this voice persisted. By 1986 she was constructing large wall sculptures and traveling weekly to New York City to film her video magazine. She was meeting famous artists like Julian Schnabel, Cindy Sherman, and Ruben Blades. Often she would meet with her director Juan Downey in his loft in the heart of SoHo. Eventually her video was completed and sold in the bookstores of the New York and Chicago art museums.

After her trips to the city she would spend days typing and editing in the small writing studio that had been my brother's room before he went away to college. The creative muse poured through her as she wrote wonderfully descriptive prose about the current art scene. Her desk was stacked with black journals filled with ideas, quotes, and pencil drawings. Alongside them were dog-eared copies of *Art in America* and *Art Digest*. At her feet was her trusted canvas L.L. Bean briefcase equipped with colored pens, writing pads, and several gallery guides. My brother's single bed, covered by a blue comforter, was always ready for his next visit.

In 1991 her work took another shift as she lost her ability to focus on large pieces. She began to contract her pieces, like the whimsical dinner plates she created with the Southwest motifs. In the spirit of Keith Herring, she played with iconic forms and colors. She spent weeks hashing out the right colors and lines for the running coyote or the standing saguaro cactus. Her studio walls were covered with various versions of these images.

She had developed a pattern of reawakening in the fall. She would become infused with creative insights, despite bouts of her body failing her and long hospital stays. Winter became the most productive time for her creative work.

But as the crocus broke through the snow outside her studio, my mother would begin to bubble up inside. The warmth would agitate her mind. She began to sleep less. She lost the ability to concentrate. Mail order catalogues covered the breakfast table. One spring she managed to order every single item in the J. Crew catalog, carefully chosen for members of the family and labeled with Post Its.

One late spring, the soaring manic behavior reached a crescendo when Jerry Brown announced his third candidacy for President. My mother thought that "Governor Moonbeam" was incredible. Day and night she was up in her studio perfecting the ultimate campaign item. She called her creation "Jerry Glasses." The sunglass frames sported a whimsical placard so wearers could prominently display "Jerry" on their foreheads. She had visions of hordes of people walking the streets of Manhattan or perhaps playing beach volleyball in Malibu, all of them eagerly wearing "Jerry" on their heads.

I was working toward my passion, too. My mind had been conditioned and filled with scientific knowledge. I began searching for graduate programs that focused on neurology.

I opened the purple and white booklet from San Francisco State University. Nothing in the biological sciences department inspired me. I started to glance at other departments. Deep within the psych department was a program labeled psychoneuroimmunology, or PNI. I began to get excited as I read the description. It focused on the connections between the brain, mind, and immune system. I picked up the phone and called Professor Saunders to schedule an informal meeting.

CHAPTER 19

Within six months I found myself moving from San Diego to San Francisco.

The geography of a place has everything to do with the temperament of the people who live there. At first glance San Diego and San Francisco seemed similar. They're both nestled on a large bay, subjected to the ebb and flow of the Pacific. As I soon discovered, however, both the cities and their residents are very different.

The relatively shallow water and gentle light in San Diego creates an environment that's laid back and meant for outdoor living. In contrast, San Francisco is always in motion. A soft, foggy wind swirls around the Victorian flats, keeping people on the go and primed for change. San Franciscans seem to welcome change. You can almost hear the collective voices cheering, "bring it on!"

The Golden Gate, symbol of the city, is literally that: a deep, narrow gate that keeps the city moving. It's strikingly beautiful but also very treacherous. In fact, it's one of the most dangerous entries into a bay in the world. The beauty seems to trump the danger. Tourists gleefully walk the bridge's span and gaze over the deep chasm, many wearing only shorts and tee shirts in the mistaken notion that it was summer here.

Setting down my belongings, I found myself entering that state of constant change. My emotional winds were blowing wildly as my mother still struggled to stay alive. Her courage inspired me. Her fear of death terrified me.

I moved in with a woman named Liz. We lived in a flat with two other women in the Mission District. Liz had the lease in her name and was renting the front room to Donna, her friend from college, and Donna's partner Kym, an organic farm worker. Kim would bring home wonderful veggies and introduced me to kale, fresh broccoli rabe, and delicata squash. Donna was studying to be a physician's assistant.

Donna was a more diligent student than I, and often I would come up with excuses to escape from my desk and interrupt her. I would recline in the warm sun in her room while she sat at her desk. Donna would briefly amuse me and then turn back to her text books. I admired her dedication.

Early one morning nine months after I arrived in San Francisco, I stood on the corner of 9th and Judah waiting for the streetcar to squeal past. I crossed the street and entered the warm light of my favorite coffee shop. I took my usual chocolate croissant and double shot latte outside and sat on the bench. I watched the commuters ride east toward the Bay Bridge. I felt the sun burning off the evening's protective blanket of fog.

The movement of warm air and water stirred my feelings. Although deep in my core I felt numb, periodically I would swell with optimism and pride in my new life. Then I would feel the fear sneaking in as I thought of the heart-shattering event that was lurking just around the corner. But today I felt only excitement, which grew with each sip of caffeine. My mother would be landing in San Francisco in two hours. She was between rounds of a new cancer therapy and was making the three-thousand mile trek to see her kids' new lives.

I drove to the airport and waited at her gate. I could feel her smile before I saw her. She was wearing a beautiful lavender scarf on her head. I gave her a big hug, her familiar smell giving me instant comfort. I took a closer look at her face. Her eyes didn't sparkle. She still didn't have any eyebrows, and her skin was dull. I gave her another hug.

The fog had returned to my neighborhood while I was at the airport. I parked the car at the B&B that was just around the corner from my flat and carried my mom's bags up the two flights of stairs.

We both flopped on the bed. She took my hand and held it tightly as we talked and laughed like old times. As she rose to freshen up in the bathroom, I picked up the phone.

"Hey, Billy, it's me. Mom arrived safely. Should we meet you at the park or do you want to come by the B&B?"

"Can you come and get me?" asked my brother, knowing his older sister would jump at the opportunity to take care of him.

"Yeah, we'll be there in 20 minutes. Mom's really excited about the concert." And I was really excited that my clan would be together.

We climbed back into my red Honda Accord, named the Red Onion. Years of four wheel off-roading had left the car smelly and unfit for transporting parents, but my mom was a good sport. I drove down Lincoln and headed downtown. My brother lived in a more urban part of San Francisco. The fog was whipping around the tops of the trees as I zipped in and out of lanes.

After we picked up Billy, we headed back toward the ocean. Golden Gate Park was softly blanketed by the dense fog. There was no wind, just a gentle hint of a breeze. We joined the crowds of people who had come from all over the peninsula to hear Santana at this free concert in the park. Within minutes, the three of us were surrounded by thousands of folks sporting colorful clothing and attitudes. I caught my brother's eye and realized we were both wondering the same thing: would Beverly be all right in this crowd of hippies?

The guitar soared and the crowd went crazy with excitement. I couldn't stand still in the presence of such seductive rhythms. My hips and arms began to sway, and my lips moved along with the lyrics.

Suddenly I felt an intense warmth on my face. I looked up. The fog had burned off to reveal a brilliant blue sky. My mood soared with the music. I was elated to be with my beloved brother and mother on this very special day.

Beverly began to dance with the pure joy that only live music can bring. Her weak and scarred body moved with abandon, like she was leaving all her fears and longings behind. Her pale face flushed and her swollen limbs moved gracefully as she drifted closer to the band. My brother and I tried to keep up with her, following her colorful scarf like it was a beacon shining in the surging, sweating crowd.

I grabbed my mother's hand and we twirled in the sun. Laughter sent golden light into my blood. With every sway of her hips, Beverly unraveled the golden cloth inside her, and soon the entire dancing audience was draped in golden thread.

We danced for nearly three hours, shedding the layers of six and a half years of heart-wrenching tension. There among the music and dancers we could finally feel free.

I dropped my brother off and drove my mother back to the B&B. She lay on the bed, humming the last song. I held her familiar hand as she drifted into a deep sleep. I sat looking out the bay window, feeling full and whole. Outside the fog was moving in again. It created a wonderful stillness. My eyes began to feel heavy. I gently lay down beside my brave mother.

When my mother was like this, I could let my compassion and love for her fill the room. When she was besieged by her demons, I focused inward, intent on getting through the next twenty-four hours and hoping that the dawn would bring her back. As this day came to a close, I felt confident that she should be fine tomorrow as well.

The next morning Mom and I piled into my car. It was July, but the fog was thick and wet. The diffuse light softened the edges of buildings, cars, and colors as I drove my red Honda a short distance to Haight Street. I was taking my mom to see Elise, whom I'd met six months earlier when she was a guest lecturer in my graduate psychology class about alternative therapies. She practiced Rosen Bodywork massage.

When I first met Elise, she had carefully explained how deeply held emotions could be released through specific touch. The body could store memory because the body was part of the brain. I listened politely but with skepticism. I believed that the brain was the only organ that stored memory and that muscles had no physiological way to store a memory. The function of a muscle was to move, not to feel.

I began seeing Elise after lectures because I was having ulcers. I thought a good massage would relax me. I had no clue that this type of bodywork would open up an entirely new world for me.

Through her massage, my body began to reveal feelings that I had tamped down. Her hands would slowly move to trigger points in my body where she would gently rest her hands. Her touch allowed the nerves in my skin and muscles to relax and release.

Soon images began to fill my mind, images that I had been too scared to look at before. As her gentle voice encouraged me to stay with the physical feelings, my body convulsed with the sadness that I had been holding deep within.

This dramatic release aroused my curious mind. This seemed like a new way to view the body. I spoke with my graduate advisor about Elise and her work. I left my advisor's office in a state of wonder. Perhaps this new field of study could begin to explain and cure my mother's pain. I might also be able to solve the mystery of my grandmother's abrupt decline. I floated down the staircase. I knew first-hand that my mother's emotional anguish was affecting her ability to fight the cancer. After every manic or suicidal episode, she would have to be hospitalized. The cancer seemed to wait until she was exhausted to spread to yet another tissue in her body.

Perhaps I could find the pathway to healing.

Elise opened the door of her brightly painted Victorian flat and let the perfumed air greet us. Inside was a world of spacious quiet. Exotic fabrics draped the walls and furniture. Unusual art was thoughtfully placed around the flat, making her home feel open, intimate, and warm.

We both took deep breaths as we walked up the wide wooden staircase to Elise's treatment room. The room faced southeast, filling the space with a warm, pink light. I sat down in the waiting area while Beverly and Elise went inside to begin her treatment. I could picture Beverly laying down her scarred fifty-three-year-old body on the table and Elise starting to move her hands over my mother's skin.

The crying began. Long, cathartic sobs that I could hear from the waiting room. The primal sounds brought tears to my eyes. As I listened, I thought about what I had learned about feelings, muscles, and the mind and hoped that my dear mom would be set free from her anguish.

My mother emerged from the session with a full spectrum of color dancing around her tired body. I recognized the grounded gait and the gritty determination in her eyes. Clearly, something had been restored in that pink room.

I held my mom's hand as we sauntered down Haight Street. The cool wind reinforced how refreshed we felt. A multitude of characters passed us on the street: old tie-dyed hippies, guitar playing musicians, bankers in suits trying to catch the downtown express, and street dogs searching for dropped bagels. I could feel the old zing in her hand as she pulled me into a bookstore.

"Marn, look at this new book by Norman Mailer. Have you read any of his work?"

I followed my mother as she weaved in and out of the bookstore aisles. The artist had found her groove in this city by the bay. Today she was whole again. Tomorrow she would board the plane for New York. The demons were gone. Beverly was back. I watched her as she read a book jacket. Her delicate dyed platinum hair was growing back in round cowlick patterns. I took a deep breath and smiled from my belly.

CHAPTER 20

It was early summer. My mother was stable. I felt confident that she wasn't at risk of dying that weekend, so my roommates and I decided to go on a backpacking trip to the Trinity Alps.

There was still snow on the peaks, but down in the meadows we were enjoying trout-filled streams, warm sunshine, and lovely wildflowers displays. I walked behind Liz and watched the insects whirl around her bandana-decorated head, rising and dipping as her steps undulated with the terrain.

Kim and I fished the cold streams with our backpacking poles. She and her father had fished many remote rivers so she was skilled at spotting good places to cast our lines. We weren't good at waiting silently for the fish to bite. We gals were always chattering about something. Liz would usually get us started. Then I would pipe in with a quick comeback. Donna would laugh in a way that would encourage the banter. Eventually Kim would steer us back to reality: catching dinner.

The third day into the trip we caught four trout. Kim cleaned them while Donna and I sat stream side, admiring her competence. We made certain to clean the fish many miles from our camp. We didn't need any carnivorous nighttime visitors looking to share our bounty.

Our base camp was under a small grove of pine in the middle of a meadow. It was one of those campsites that make you feel immediately at ease. I could see far down to the end of the meadow, the direction we had come from. To the north and south I could also see the boundaries of this great meadow and the steep cliffs climbing over our heads. The late afternoon sun lit up the granite rock about a hundred yards away.

Liz and I shared a tent. She would stay up late traveling vast fictional universes in the Star Wars Trilogy while I would drift off into a light sleep. I liked camp sleep. It was different from sleeping inside in a safe bed. Outside my sleep ears listened to the wind around me, ready to awaken me if they detected an intruder. I could also gaze at the night sky through the mesh, the stars slowly passing by.

Liz and I were similar in many ways. Both of us had grown up on the East Coast and had found a new and exciting life in the West. She also had a wild Scorpio streak in her that I could relate to. Often I would clutch her around the waist while riding on the back of her Honda motorcycle. We would whiz through the foggy streets of San Francisco, surging up and down into neighborhoods filled with sizzling noodles, oven baked pizzas, or Hot and Hunky hamburgers. We were both exploring the limits of our personalities, and it had created a deep bond between us.

On the fifth day of our backpacking trip, we hiked out of the meadow into a wooded area and set up camp on the banks of a clear mountain stream. We stayed up late, talking under the starlight. I felt deeply relaxed and at home among my friends, the pine cones, and the granite rocks. I stood up and said good night. I lay back gently on my tired back and gazed at the pine branches through my tent mesh. Slowly I drifted into a soothing sleep.

That night my mom came to me in a dream. I was sitting by a gentle stream, dipping my fingers in and out of the water. I heard her say, "You must come home." Her voice was clear and grounded. I looked at her face and understood that this wasn't merely a dream. The colors around me were muted like in real life. She touched my shoulder and gave me a loving squeeze before she walked back into the woods.

I woke up disoriented. I rubbed my face to feel my flesh. I knew that my mom needed me to be with her before she died. Without hesitation I woke up Liz, Donna, and Kim and told them that we had to break camp. In the pre-dawn hours they scrambled to stuff their bags, fold their tents, and pack their backpacks. In thirty minutes we were on the trail. For the first time we walked in silence.

When we arrived home, there was a message on my answering machine that my father had left the night before. He instructed me to come home. My mother was in the hospital, and he hoped that I would make it back before she died. I caught the red eye flight to JFK.

The time in the air gave me a chance to reflect. Up until then I had believed that there was some way to save her. Not necessarily save her physical body from dying but save her dignity. I had thought that there must be something I could say or do that would help her cope with this total collapse of life.

Now I was at a loss. All of Beverly's suffering to stay alive seemed so futile at this moment.

What was the meaning of these long years of suffering? Why do life forms have such attachments to a bunch of atoms? Why would my mother, this collection of molecules, ultimately care so much about the fate of the vessel she was in? Why did I?

My mother had an intense desire to live, and she fought with every strand of will in her body. So it wasn't just dust to dust. She, whoever she was, had an attachment to this dust. She did not want to give up that unique arrangement of molecules to become some other arrangement. As I thought about sitting at my mother's deathbed, I felt ill-equipped to take care of her fears or to take care of mine.

I walked into the hospital room to find my brother, his wife, and my father at her side. My father and brother looked drained. My sister-in-law and I, having just arrived, were rested and ready to stay the entire night. We gave hugs and the guys went home.

I walked to my mom's bedside and sat as close to her as I could. I held her hand for countless hours. She winced and groaned with primal sounds. I focused on her face. Her eyes were closed. Periodically she would knock her head with a closed fist in an angry, frantic motion. Around her right eye and forehead was a large, green bruise.

I tried talking to her. She would go in and out of consciousness. Stroking her hand, I softly encouraged her to give in to the inevitable, to let go of life and free herself of this unbelievable suffering. Her physical body was crumbling like a brittle, dry leaf, but her will was still as strong as a bull. She twisted and thrashed, desperate to fight off the unwinding of her.

I was preparing myself for the moment that she would cease to exist. I believed that when the moment came, she would just stop like a car that had run out of gas. Everything would just stop.

But that's not what happened.

While I was holding her hand, I felt, and perhaps saw, her lift away. The buzz in her hand that I had felt a moment before rose above her body and drifted out.

I was stunned.

I was relieved.

The hand that I was still holding suddenly felt more like a piece of wood than my mother's hand. My hands held the dust, but there was something more. It seemed to hover above her body. I couldn't see it with my eyes, but I saw it with my inner eye. It was white and had the energetic embodiment of Beverly Gay

Wilde. There was something left from the dust and it seemed to find a home.

Beverly had gone somewhere. I didn't know where. I certainly didn't have a heavenly name for it, but I had the comfort of "her" being somewhere magical and unexpected.

As quickly as the white energy appeared, it was gone. It was at this moment that I wept.

What I thought was Beverly, the physical body, was left as a corpse on the bed. Beverly was vastly larger than that. The essence of her did not perish. Instead it appeared to be cut free. She was liberated.

My mother's illness had drawn out for seven long years. Even with the removal of both of her breasts, leaving horrifying, deep scars, the cancer spread to her lymph system. The cancer then used the lymphatic system as a way to travel throughout her body.

At times when I would see my mother I couldn't imagine the physical body being able to survive such torture. There were many times along that journey that she nearly died, but by sheer will she came through the gates with incredible force.

Standing at the window of my parent's bedroom after the funeral, I fell to my knees in deep sorrow. I sobbed while gazing out the window. I yearned for my mother's flesh. I had witnessed Beverly's flight, but I was still in the physical world and the family's energy had been sucked away with her. The room was brightly lit, but it felt like a dank and lightless hole. My despair was so utterly deep. I never imagined that the heart could feel so heavy.

CHAPTER 21

"This is just great!" I yelled sarcastically, as I searched for my car in the Mills College parking lot. I finally spotted the black Pontiac Grand Am with dual exhaust. It was my mom's car. I had driven it across the country this past summer after my mom's funeral.

I got in and sat in the parking lot, wiping away tears of anger. I was livid.

Jennifer's betrayal only confirmed what I knew to be true: the entire universe was heartless. I had met her six months before my mother died, dated her after my mother's death, and now my affection for her was growing. Clearly she didn't feel the same way.

I had sat on her bed in her beautiful dark wood Mills College dorm room. I was expecting to have a nice lunch date. Instead she confessed that she had slept with her soccer pal last night on the same bed.

I drove out of the parking lot and headed toward the Bay Bridge, the Indigo Girls blaring on the stereo. Midway across the bridge, I drove into the iconic San Francisco fog. Immediately I felt its dominance and my own insignificance.

This souped-up sports car knew only one speed: fast. It was part of my mom's last hoorah when she was dying. She had dyed her hair platinum blond and would roar around the small towns of Pound Ridge and Mount

Kisco, New York with NPR playing on the radio. This car was her rebellion.

Armored with the power of anger, I flew across the majestic Bay Bridge. The cold light reflecting off the steel hardened my resolve to clamp down on my growing anguish. I felt a deep disgust for the world.

"May it all turn to steel!" I screamed at the huge support that rose out of the bay.

I had been sinking further and further into a deep, narrow pit since Beverly's death. This breakup was the last straw. There was nothing left to keep me from plunging all the way to the bottom.

The energetic end of my downward spiral came a moment later. Just before the Fell Street exit, brake lights suddenly flashed in front of me. I knew before I hit the car that it was going to be a horrific accident.

All sound stopped as I plowed into the car in front of me. Seconds later I felt my entire body thrust forward as I was smashed from behind by a car going even faster than I was.

I sat there in astonishment. Such a dramatic change in such a contracted space of time. One moment I was driving along belting out the cathartic lyrics, "It's only life after all," and the next I was caught in a chain of events that was completely out of my control.

I sat in the bizarre stillness of the calamity's aftermath, staring at the broken glass scattered over the black asphalt.

I heard a knock on the window.

"Are you ok?" asked a young woman with wide, piercing eyes.

"Yes," I said with a nod.

She walked to the car behind me, and I realized that she must have been the driver who hit me. I replayed our brief conversation. It meant that I was alive. I would be eternally grateful to her for pointing out this fact to me.

Knowing that I was alive gave me the courage to assess my body. I felt my face. My skin didn't feel wet. Good, no blood. I scanned my hands. They were still holding the steering wheel. Slowly I moved a finger and then the entire hand. I took a deep breath and wiggled my entire body.

Fine, I'm fine. I can get out of this car. I'll be fine, I said to myself, checking my cognitive abilities.

As I opened the car door, I looked into the car in front of me. I could see the occupants moving in their seats. They too were alive and trying to get out. I climbed out and sat on the curb.

I stared at my car in amazement. It was destroyed. Only the seat I had been singing in was untouched. It was as if this car had sacrificed itself in order to save me. As if my mother's car had wrapped around me like a protective blanket and allowed me to survive a near death experience.

I took in the light glinting off the twisted steel. Earlier my eyes had found kinship with this light. Now I looked at the metal with a blank dullness. I was alive, yes, but numb to the life within me. I stood up slowly, not feeling any part of my body.

I stumbled along the asphalt of the freeway. Masses of crumpled, mangled cars filled my entire visual field. Rescue workers moved among the stunned survivors, their presence like a spoonful of honey, reminding us of life's sweetness.

In a daze I walked through Golden Gate Park toward home, slowly placing one foot in front of the other. The cool air helped brush off some of the horror. By the time I arrived at my flat, I was exhausted and beginning to feel the pain throughout my body. I climbed the long staircase and fell into the blue futon in the living room. I stared out of the bay window into the limbs of the cypress tree.

Donna had heard me come in. Her footsteps, softened with slippers, approached me.

"Marn, are you ok?"

"I'm not sure," I answered, reaching my hand out to her. "I feel funny."

She sat on the edge of the futon and touched me on the shoulder. Donna was a big-hearted, nurturing type. The house cat Pico jumped in her lap. She stroked both of us. Her girlfriend Kym came and joined us. She touched me on the head.

"I'll make you a cup of chamomile tea, Marn," Kym declared in her self-assured voice.

I breathed deeply and felt my body begin to relax. I was in good hands here with my dear friends. I began to tell the story. Liz joined us and we sat for an hour discussing the huge crash.

Suddenly my entire body felt numb and sleepy. I wanted to lay my head down, but Donna insisted that I stay awake in case I had a concussion. Despite the love of these dear friends, I felt as crumpled as the car I had just left on the freeway.

Monday morning the insurance company called and confirmed what I already knew: the car had been totaled. My mother's car would be hauled off to a wrecking yard.

The harsh reality hit me in the stomach. Beverly was physically gone. This was the end of the car, the end of her. Junkyards and graveyards are both dead ends.

I was at a dead end as well. I left like I was sitting on the bottom of a deep pit. The darkness felt good, and I didn't want to leave. I enjoyed hanging out there. I wanted to drink from smelly bars, eat greasy food, and bath only twice a week. I liked the heap of laundry growing in my closet.

I didn't know that settling into this pit would create a dangerous addiction. I liked it down here, but, as I soon found out, liking it would make it almost impossible to climb back out.

CHAPTER 22

The clatter of the six a.m. N Judah streetcar woke me every weekday morning. I lived in a railroad flat two blocks from Golden Gate Park. The flat was old and couldn't keep out the damp cold of the coastal fog that gathered every morning. It was too cold to hang out in my bedroom or in the kitchen with Kym, Liz or Donna, so I would venture out onto the humming streets looking for coffee.

There were several neighborhood cafes filled with sleepy graduate or medical students. Many of them would stumble inside with bed heads and their night clothes still warm from their wool blankets. I felt at home with this crowd. The grouchy English major sipping Earl Grey gave me license to wallow in my own distrust and dismay at the unforgiving world around me.

The double latte warmed my hands as I carefully walked across the busy Lincoln Boulevard and into the majestic forest that is Golden Gate Park. I stopped to gaze up at the cypress trees swaying like sea weed in the thick fog. I watched with interest, but, in my morose state of mind, the beauty of the scene escaped me.

The Botanical Gardens in the Park was home to a wonderful grove of redwood trees that I would visit weekly. Jennifer had introduced me to this secluded site. We would sit on the bench and hold hands. Today I sat beneath them, hoping to absorb some of their wisdom. I felt their quiet, steady nature, but my mind couldn't summon the energy to engage with these majestic teachers. Instead I sat and sat in a dull silence, waiting for change to happen to me. Eventually I walked back to my flat to resume working on my master's thesis.

I was exploring the relationship between the physical body and the emotional body by looking at the hormone cortisol. Cortisol was known to be associated with stress and also to have an inter-relationship with the physical and emotional. I had constructed a study to look at the salivary levels of cortisol before and after Rosen Method massage.

But my heart wasn't in it. My mother's illness had been the impetus for my course of study. Now that my mother was dead, I had lost my motivation. My conclusions would not bring Beverly back to life.

One morning about six weeks after the accident, I was sitting in a lecture with about 30 other students. We were learning about terminal illness and the emotional effects of confronting dying. I looked around the room. Students were listening intently. I was shaken. I had just lived through this and effectively buried it.

Suddenly the room became very narrow, and I felt as if I were floating above it. The teacher's voice was muted. The colors around me lost their significance. I needed to leave. Not just the room but my entire experience. I wanted an entirely different venue. Maybe Saturn or Venus. Anywhere but here. I felt desperate.

I stood up and quickly walked toward the door. I felt for the knob, and when I had it in my hand I focused my entire consciousness on turning it clockwise so that I could have some space. I heard a muffled voice call out my name, but I ignored it. It felt like a miracle when I found myself in the hallway.

I rested with my back against the cold cement wall and began to relax. I thought that perhaps it was just a fleeting moment of panic. But like a tidal wave the panic washed over me again. The feeling was unbearable. I needed to escape. I looked desperately up and down the hallway for a bathroom.

Inside the bathroom I splashed cold water on my face and tried to talk myself down. *Okay, I'm still alive. I'm right here in this bathroom,* I reassured myself, trying to affirm my very existence on the planet.

The door opened and I was surrounded by young female chatter. The human activity was reassuring, but I didn't want to see anyone. Quickly, without a care for how I looked, I tucked myself away into a stall and sat on the toilet for a very long time. Sweat was rolling down my back and my palms were clammy. I felt terrible.

Over the next two years, this out-of-body experience became a frequent visitor. It would hit me at any moment. I could always tell it was coming on. I would feel this expansion beyond my physical self, as if I were floating above my own body. I had the sensation of being out of my body and viewing myself from the outside. It was eerie.

I learned to carry on, acting as if things were normal. But I was always waiting for the next wave of anxiety. I became afraid of being alone but terrified of social situations because words or circumstances would set me off. I worried that I would have a heart attack. I was terrified of my classes but didn't feel that dropping out was an option. I was terrified of doctors because I feared that I was losing my mind or dying of cancer and didn't want to know.

At first I tried to fight it. When I felt myself turning into a hot air balloon floating above my day-to-day activities, I would try desperately to anchor myself. As time went on, however, I began to find comfort in it. What a great way to escape.

And then I became capable of inducing the experience. It became an addiction, this desire to escape the pain of life. No longer were the attacks unconscious; now I found them as the only way to cope with my disjointed ideas about life and death.

Expansion.

Contraction.

To cope with emotional pain, I learned to expand beyond my emotions. Just like when a person goes into shock after a car accident and feels high and disconnected from herself. I was in a constant state of flight or fight. I learned to collapse in. I began to hide in my room more, to decline social engagements. I liked the dark, quiet and predictable space that was my bedroom.

I had no idea how to deal with grief.

CHAPTER 23

The grief after my mother's death blasted apart what remained of my family. My brother moved from San Francisco to Sacramento with his partner Jen. He was adrift and thought law school might fit. Within a year, my father remarried and lived in the family home in New York. His alliance with his new family caused a deep slash in my bond with my father. We were holding on by a thread.

I felt adrift as well and dug my toes into the sand of the only home I had: San Francisco. Like she had done with so many other lost souls, she took me in, nurtured my heart, and eventually set me free as a whole, grounded person.

I sat at the small tea table I had rescued from the trash. I was eating fresh sautéed chard with soy sauce and looking out the round window that over-looked a deep green garden. A dim light shone from the corner of the room. The room felt safe and cozy. Perhaps it was the incense wafting from the room next door or the soothing sound of the street car that rattled the flat as it passed in the distance. Or perhaps it was the echo of all the other souls who had come to San Francisco to find safety and themselves.

The morning was cold and foggy. I shuffled into our turquoise blue kitchen and headed straight to the rainbow painted ceramic pot. It was filled with dark and aromatic French coffee, roasted by a coffee master just around the corner on 9th Avenue. I ground the beans and stared sleepily into the billowing fog outside the back window. I liked the harsh taste of French roast, its bitterness being the only taste my tongue cared to sense.

I was still groggy from the night's adventure. I had been in the kitchen five hours earlier, awakened by the sound of intruders. They turned out to be large raccoons crawling on the kitchen floor and cabinets.

I felt like I was in a Lawrence Durrell novel, living among wild animals, although the nearest wilds were in Golden Gate Park, one block away. I looked down to the end of the long narrow kitchen and saw that the back door was wide open.

It's not easy to relocate raccoons. They're bigger than in Walt Disney films. They have very solid arched backs, and their swagger means business. Finally, after making my voice harsh and my body tall, I had come out the winner. I had fallen back into bed, exhausted from over sizing myself.

The coffee dripped from the Melitta filter into a ceramic mug I had made ten years earlier at the Grove Center on the UCSD campus. The handle still felt right in my hand as I drew the first sip of my morning nectar. I needed my energy boost. Today was Saturday, and my roommates and I were off to mountain bike the bobcat trail in the Marin Headlands.

The trail wasn't very challenging. It slowly rose from sea level to a ridge top, giving the rider a spectacular view of the bay. If we went early enough in the morning, we could see bobcats heading home from their nocturnal journeys, their fluid motions echoing the valley's contours.

I truly enjoyed this trail. It took me far away from the dull ache in my head. At times I would imagine that I was in Scotland among the heathers. When I rode with Liz or Kym, we would compete with each other and end our ride exhausted and ready for a super carne asada burrito, filling our bellies with meat, beans, sour cream, cheese, salsa and avocado.

Other times I would ride by myself. I felt the strain on my calves. I wiped the sweat from my brow. I felt my lungs draw in the moist sea air and my heart move my chest in and out as it worked hard to keep me alive.

I felt as ungrounded as the black birds I would watch darting in and out of the swampy meadow, negotiating the winds over their nests. My spirit heart was terribly bruised. I had no anchor. In the past I had held onto the idea that life had meaning. That life fit into a neat box of scientific reasoning. That events happened in nature because of survival of the fittest, entropy, and chance.

All my mind could perceive now was the absurd cruelty of life.

Later that week, I was sitting in the Botanical Gardens reading the *Sunday New York Times*. I came across an article in the magazine section about a dozen women who lived in the Los Angeles area. All of them were Vietnamese, and all of them were blind. They could detect no light at all. Each of them, independent of each other, had sought the advice of an ophthalmologist. The eye doctor was perplexed. There was nothing wrong with their eyes physiologically. She was at a loss for an explanation.

Serendipitously she described these patients to a friend who was a social worker. Her friend offered to talk to some of the women. It didn't take her long to make the connection. Every single one of them had seen their families murdered before their eyes. Their eyes had seen the horrible brutality that only war can bring. As a result, each woman was unwilling and unable to see. Their sensory organs were intact and without disease; it was their emotions that were blocking the light.

After several months of therapy, revisiting the emotional memories associated with what their eyes recorded, each woman was able to see again. The emotional obstructions were gone.

The article struck a deep chord. I ripped it out of the magazine and tucked it into my backpack. I reflected on my mom. I wondered if all of the years she struggled with manic depression might have weakened her ability to fight off cancer cells. Perhaps I would be able to uncover the logical rationale for all of her suffering.

I also thought about blindness. I didn't know why, but just the word "blind" seemed to punch me in the stomach. I couldn't imagine how this article might relate to me. I didn't understand how Beverly and I had both been unable to make sense of loss. My own panic attacks and depression were simply the clothing I wore. It didn't occur to me that I could change them. And I certainly didn't know that I would begin to lose the gift my mother gave me, the gift of light and color.

I tilted my head back and gazed up at the branches of the majestic Monterey cyprus tree I was sitting under. I peered into the shadowy places among the limbs high above my head and thought about the mysterious things that can live in shadow. I watched how the daylight made the blue green needles glimmer. I marveled at the simple beauty brought forth in the contrast. Light needs dark.

A visual memory suddenly flashed.

Every bone in her face was broken by her abusive husband. It was hard to tell a human lived behind such a swollen mass. As difficult as this was to see, it was the anguish in her eyes that I would never forget. She was crazy, of course; that's why she was in the mental hospital with my mother. But it was the sane glimmer in her eyes that caught me, a brief connection that tied us together for an instant.

Her image was tattooed in the depths of my brain. It was stored there alongside the sight of my mother collapsed with her head propped up by the steering wheel in the SUNY Purchase parking lot, her mouth gaping and looking as if she had already signed a contract with death.

I heard a hawk overhead. I watched it circle in the sky. The movement shifted my attention, and I began to wonder about eyes.

Eyes are organs of perception. The retinal cells take wavelengths of light and convert them into a series of chemical messages. These messages are then relayed to the cortical parts of the brain in order to interpret what the light represents. Thus my eyes need light. My eyes exist because of light. Light is stimulation and food for my eyes.

But the quality of light differs. Light emerging from a mountain meadow caresses my retinal cells. Light from my mother's tear-swollen face does not. My eyes have seen horror. These images of horror are forever part of my brain.

CHAPTER 24

My alarm clock broadcasted the voices of NPR into my
bedroom. I shuffled into the bathroom and looked into
the mirror. My face looked as foggy and sleepy as my
brain felt. Then my eyes came into focus. The beam of
consciousness danced back and forth from the mirror to
my eyes and to my mind. Back and forth.

What am I? Who am I?

How do I know that I am?

I stared at my face in the mirror and bit my lip
to affirm my existence.

The questioning was exhausting. I was desperate to find some way out of this hole, out of this bleak
existence.

Six months earlier, while I still worked at
Noah's Bagels, a customer gave me an announcement of
her upcoming class. It was a class on spiritual matters. I
had saved it on my desk.

As I walked back into my room I saw the flyer
sitting there.

Lucky for me, I thought. *The class starts in four days.*

I opened the large redwood door to a candlelit
roomful of students. Tonight was my first spiritual class.
It was called "Inner Life." I didn't know what to expect,
but I had met the teacher months earlier in a Chinese
medicine class at the community college, and she had
impressed me with her knowledge. I was skeptical, but I

told myself that it was just a class. I certainly had no intention in doing any of this stuff myself.

The warm candlelight soothed my eyes. The twelve other students were sitting on pillows, reclining in cushy chairs and couches, or sitting upright in rocking chairs. I found a cozy spot in the middle of a mahogany leather couch. Students on both sides of me turned and smiled.

The room was filled with color. As I took out my notebook and opened it to a fresh page, a painting above the fireplace caught my attention. It was radiant. An Asian woman was sitting cross-legged among billowing clouds. I felt her looking directly at me with soft, kind eyes. I was familiar with post modern abstract paintings, but this particular painting evoked a different kind of relationship between the viewer and the image. I felt as if I could stare at her for hours.

Beyond the living room was a narrow hallway where I could see the teacher opening a jar on one of the shelves. She pulled out a handful of yellow wooden sticks. On the shelves were hundreds of jars labeled in Chinese and filled with medicinal herbs, each throwing rich warm rays of colors toward me. Apparently this was her herbal apothecary.

People were chatting as we waited for the class to start. I slowly surveyed the room. Behind me were bookcases bursting with leather-bound books, the shelves heavy with old knowledge. To my left was a curious etching of a ladder with circles where the rungs met. Hebrew letters were written in the circles and on the rungs. Like the painting over the fireplace, this picture clearly had a purpose to it. I just didn't know what it was.

The teacher Susan Kaplan walked into the room and began greeting us. She was a petite, dark-haired, older Jewish woman. I felt my shoulders tighten. This was a mysterious world to me, and I was a little scared to peer behind the curtain.

"Hello, everyone. Thanks for coming to this class. Please take one of these handouts as I gather my notes and materials for tonight," she said, with a distinct Brooklyn accent.

My shoulders loosened up and I smiled. I knew that I had nothing to worry about. A woman from Brooklyn was someone I could easily feel at home with. I could smell The Strand bookstore and realized what this room reminded me of: a comfortable old bookstore on the lower east side of Manhattan or Green Apple Books on Clement Street in San Francisco.

This room is filled with subjects I know nothing about. I'm about to embark on a true adventure.

Susan sat in her rocking chair with an air of self-confidence that comes from years of living and searching for the painful and joyous truths of life. I would soon learn just how blessed I was to have such a wonderful teacher for these mystery studies.

Over the course of several months we explored worlds I didn't know existed. We studied such topics as the Four Elements, the Tree of Life, chakras, and mandalas. Slowly I began to see that cultures all over the world had beautiful and elaborate maps to make sense of the terrifying crisis I was having. Each map offered a different way to explore the unknowable, the meaning of our existence.

For the first time in my life, I was able to gaze without judgment at many of these spiritual traditions. I began to think that I might be able to understand where Beverly went that day she died. I began to realize that thousands of years of human knowledge must have distilled something immensely more poetic than the current reductionist molecular model I had.

So I took a chance and dove into these new studies. At times I found the worlds these traditions described bizarre and freaky. We discussed stories of yogis that could live years on only water, Taoist monks who were mummified vessels that were still breathing, or the angels Gabriel and Raphael as real beings. I was beginning to explore the "dream world," a world that couldn't be explained by evidence, only from stories and direct experience.

Fear would wash over me as I sat in class, but I was desperate for a new road to follow. Often I would calm my fear by taking a deep breath and looking around the classroom, conjuring up the smell of the old used bookstore. The rich tones and candlelight shadows eased my racing heart.

They're just ideas. That's all. I can always discard them if I don't like them.

In the class was a very tall, exotic looking woman. Her long, thick black hair swung as she rose from the chair to get a cup of tea. Her voice was as bold as the clothes she wore. Draped over her knees was a sweater that was a symphony of reds, yellows and blues. Underneath her sweater was a worn pair of Levi's supported by a wide leather belt. I would sit where I could observe her from across the room. I studied her confidence, the solid grace that she presented to the world and that I so sorely lacked. She seemed like she had seen wild and alien things that had made her strong.

At our last class of the series we gathered to perform a ritual. I had never done a ritual before, but I wasn't afraid. I had grown confident that I wasn't in some cult and that my mind wouldn't snap from too much esoteric knowledge. Instead I was beginning to feel like I had some new tools to work with that might build my new road. Life had begun to feel expansive, curious, and light-filled.

For the ritual Susan instructed us to bring a cross-cultural item to share with the group. She requested that the item have a deep connection to the owner. I hesitated to bring *Vanishing Africa*, because it seemed corny to bring a book. But it was my favorite book, and it kept coming into my mind when I thought about what to share.

I loved this photo book. When I was a young child my mother and I spent countless hours snuggled on our gray couch flipping through the pages, lost in the pictures of African tribes. Even then I was struck with the beauty and intimacy they had with the natural world around them. The book was like a piece of clothing I shared with my mother. A scarf that we both wore around our necks, and it held her smell and my smell.

In class that day we all sat in a circle on the floor around a cloth of an incredible deep purple. Students brought out their items and shared them one by one. I felt my face flush when I began to share my book with the class.

The tall, dark woman interrupted me. " Marney, turn the book over so that we can see the author and photographer."

She spoke with such authority that I immediately did as she asked.

The author's face was very familiar because my mother and I used to look at her and wonder about her and her life as an artist.

"That's my mother," she said softly. "I was a young child when she created this book. I was in Africa with her when she took all the pictures."

I was stunned. "This is my favorite book that my mom and I read together. I can't believe the coincidence!"

The teacher gently refocused the class to continue to share their objects. The woman sitting across from me continued to smile and warm my heart. I felt a velvet string moving from my heart to hers. It was strong, like a mother's grip on your hand as you cross a busy street.

Then I became very still and let a fragrance blanket me. It was the unmistakable smell of my mother. *Mother, yes mother.* My heart raced as I allowed every molecule of that smell to touch me. I could feel my body fill up. *I am not alone. She is here.*

I couldn't believe the gift that was bestowed upon me that day. A new journey was beginning. I never saw the mysterious woman again, but the depth of that experience fermented in me. I was beginning to live from my gut instincts. My teachers and lessons would be arriving in various forms, often unconventional, and I was learning to listen and surrender.

CHAPTER 25

When I opened the back door to the old California ranch house, the warm, spicy air touched me like a caress. I could smell green tea, soy sauce, and star anise as I stepped forward to give my new teacher Charles Belyea a delicate hug. He walked toward me like a sheet in the wind, barely touching the ground. Then he gracefully turned and lowered the volume on his stereo, relegating the Chinese opera to the background.

It was eight in the morning, and Susan and I were the first to arrive. The small class was an introduction to the Tao Te Ching. Susan, my friend and previous teacher, had introduced me to this class. Aside from a teacher of spiritual traditions, she was also an accomplished acupuncturist. She was excited to attend Charles' new class and thought that I would find it helpful. Charles had studied Taoism in Taiwan in the seventies. When he returned to America, he founded and directed the Five Branches Institute College of Traditional Chinese Medicine in Santa Cruz.

When the other eight students had arrived, we gathered in the spacious kitchen. Charles had prepared congee, steamed pork buns, sliced persimmons, and a steaming pork dish. As we ate and sipped green tea Charles told us whimsical stories about his life. By mid morning we had full bellies and were ready for our monthly lesson on the ancient Taoist teachings.

Months earlier I had taken my first spiritual class at Susan's, I was ready for more in-depth study. I had always had an appreciation for Chinese culture and was anxious to explore it. This class was my first exposure to Chinese cultural philosophy and the beginning of what would become an intensive two-year journey into the world of Taoism, a world filled with exquisite poetry, elaborate cognitive maps, beautiful brush paintings, and a new cosmology.

The Tao, the original mother of all living things, became my mother.

Charles sat at the head of the table with several books opened in front of him. We began the session by talking about how our meditation practice had gone during the month. All of us were finding it to be difficult. Thankfully Charles was patient.

The instructions were simple. I was to sit in a quiet room and focus on the area just below my navel. When my mind wandered, I should just bring my concentration back to that spot. It was the simplicity of the instructions that made this exercise so difficult. The illusive poetry of the Tao Te Ching is the instruction manual for Taoist meditation. The text we were instructed to read every morning illustrated the immense difficulty in focusing one's mind and breath. After meditating, we were to sit for an hour, trying to let go and forget everything.

During the first six months I found the journey of stillness to be a difficult trek. Besides the normal chatter of my mind, emotional storms would brew. Sometimes I would obsess over the numbness in my legs. Other mornings my mind would be distracted by thoughts of the donut I was craving. I often felt like a failure. But when I would return to class, our teacher would remind us that it's called *practicing* meditation.

The discipline of doing nothing was the most difficult task I had ever dedicated myself to. But within the difficulty were small glimmers of my former self and something beyond that.

Sitting all alone in my room in San Francisco, I began to feel connected to the woods of my past and my heartbeat in the present moment. The beating of my heart would terrify me. The simplicity of the sound of my life. Without this sound, I was dead. My existence felt frail.

The readings suggested that I could experience a thread of connection. I tried, contorting my mind to expand, but I only felt isolated in my physical obsessions. My mind would drift toward the pain in my shoulder or the rent that was due.

Out of respect for ancient and mysterious culture, I persevered. For an entire month, I would read the same small poem over and over again. The lines would dance in front of me as I commuted to my job at the health food store.

Over time I became very connected to each monthly poem. They seemed to become songs and held a certain resonance with me.

Then I was given a gift.

It lasted all of a minute, but its impact has served me a lifetime.

I was riding to work on the N Judah line. This trolley is above ground and winds noisily through the foggy streets of San Francisco's sunset district. I had just read the Tao Te Ching passage for the month. It was wonderfully mysterious.

To see the small is called 'illuminated perception.'
To abide in the delicate is called 'strength.'
If you use the outer rays to return to the bright inner light,
Your life will be preserved.
This is called following the 'always so.'

Translated by Charles Belaey

I had read the same set of lines for 25 days. I still didn't understand the words, but it felt like their sounds and rhythm had become a part of me. Suddenly, without fanfare, a magic portal opened, and my perception shifted to another aspect of the world. For a fleeting moment the entire trolley reflected the quality of movement the Taoist passage was referring to. The trolley car, the flowers outside, the passengers, even the occasional fly were all dancing to the same song, all swaying to the same rhythm. Time became endless. Everything was with everything, just distinctly its own. It was wonderful, and I felt for the first time in my life deeply connected to life. Time and space became irrelevant and only the energetic resonance remained.

It was gone in a flash.

I felt renewed. I was left with a new understanding of the experiences around me. My atoms were not my atoms but rather skirted and drifted about. There was a dancing interplay between all the atoms within the trolley. Nothing was fixed, nothing was attached. Instead of feeling lonely or lost in this sea of chaos and movement, I felt like I was in good company.

The knowledge I had acquired about chemistry, physics and biology was illuminated in 3-D at that brief moment. I didn't need to reject my past. Instead, I saw how all knowledge is a face on a multi-dimensional cube.

Slowly over the course of two years, I began an internal transformation and acceptance into a natural world I could not perceive. It was a world full of non absolutes and acceptance of the "as is."

From a Taoist perspective, the energetic flow of nature is always there. We only need to affirm our ability to hear and feel it. One can never lose the Great Mother, but one can never fully name her, either. Instead we can find comfort in the mystery. I was being taught to be fully present to the moment, where I would find the Great Mother, the Tao.

I am nature and she is within me. The exploration allowed me to go back to my past when I was young and innocent, with an unadulterated view of my place in nature. Now, as an adult, I could reconnect to the splendor of nature but also hold the mystery as a mystery, "the always so." I could let go of the inquisitive mind of the scientist and embrace a new mystery. For the first time I felt one of the basic laws of science. Energy is neither created nor destroyed.

CHAPTER 26

I heard the motorcycle rev in the garage below. It was a small Honda, perfect for Liz's five-foot-four frame. I quickly put on my leather jacket and ran down the long flight of stairs. I walked into the garage to see Liz straddled on the bike. I jumped on and she confidently pulled out of the garage.

We were racing off to meet Kim and Donna at The Café in the Castro. I had just gotten off work and was ready to have a beer. Liz and I walked upstairs into a spacious bar. Kim was at the back of the bar bent over a game of pool. Donna was sitting nearby on a stool, waiting for her turn. I walked up to Donna and wrapped my arm around her to say hello.

Kim made her shot and gave me a soft shoulder bump. Laughing, I bumped her back. Liz joined in, bumping Kim on the other shoulder. While the three of us jostled, Donna sank a ball into the corner pocket.

"You better pay attention, Kim. Donna is kickin' your butt over there," I goaded Kim, giving her one last shove.

"I'm not worried," Kim boasted. "Donna has never beaten me."

"Hey, Liz, grab me a beer, too," I said over my shoulder, as Liz walked toward the bar.

I sat down and watched the lovers play pool. They were laughing and having a great time. Donna waved her stick in front of Kim to distract her. Kim rolled her eyes in feigned annoyance. The playful teasing created an air of romance that was lovely to watch.

Liz returned from the bar and sat next to me. I felt my body relax as I listened to the music blasting on the sound system. This clan of women was my family now. I sank what little I had left of myself here with this good tribe of women. We were all queer outcasts trying to find our way in this city of refuge.

"Thanksgiving's just a week away so we better start planning," Liz announced. "I want to bake two pies. Kim said she would pick up chard, carrots, and potatoes from work."

Liz was an amazing cook, and her love of food reminded me of my mother. Beverly would spend hours fussing over the details of a big meal. Liz, like her, approached the table like a work of art.

"I really want to make the stuffing. I can get a good turkey from the Inner Sunset Co-op," I said, with growing enthusiasm. This would be my second Thanksgiving with them. Last year I had no taste for food, but I was pleasantly surprised to find myself looking forward to this simple pleasure again.

When the day arrived we all got up early to start preparing our dishes. I walked into the parlor and put a Frank Sinatra record on the stereo. This was going to be a grand day. Blenders were whirling, carrots were getting sliced, apples cut, bread crumbs were soaking, and table clothes were being ironed. At three o'clock we were ready. The table was filled with carefully prepared food.

Other wayward friends arrived, and soon the room was brimming with affection. Each guest brought a gift of food or drink draped in affection. There was such a generosity of spirit that I felt myself coming alive again. The smell of savory stuffing made my stomach ache with pleasure. The rich reds of the wine, candles, cranberry sauce, and tablecloth cloaked me in warmth. The joy in Donna's eyes as she sliced the perfect turkey flooded me with a feeling of belonging.

I sat back in my chair after the exquisite meal. This day, after two years in free fall, I felt that I could survive the crushing grief. The air was crisp and damp outside, making the window misty. Inside this cozy flat, music played, friends laughed, and I was warm inside and out. Donna and Kim had moved to the blue futon and were snuggled like two kittens. I smiled to myself. *I have a good home.*

*   *   *

Grounded in this loving home I was able to find a new friend that brought the light back into my heart. Her name was Suzanne, but I would eventually call her Sparky.

Petite but strong, Suzanne had the presence of a cashmere goat. She was tough like a goat, ready to navigate the rocky terrain of life. At the same time she was soft, warm and beautiful. But what attracted me to her most was her dedication to living a meaningful life. She taught me that life was worth living if one could find the gift one wanted to give back.

I met her at my new job. I was on break from Noah's Bagels and had bought my lunch at the Inner Sunset Co-op. Noshing on my veggie sprout sandwich, I stood reading the bulletin board. An ad caught my eye: "Become a Worker-Owner at Other Avenues Food Co-op."

Within two weeks I had been interviewed and offered a job. I was delighted to leave the bagel shop and transition into becoming an owner of a collectively owned health food store.

"Come on, Marn! It's 12:30. The meeting is starting," yelled Suzanne from the coolers in the front of the store.

I watched her grab a wedge of goat brie cheese with her free hand. In the other hand she had a jar of strawberry jam. Wedged under her arm and snug against her body was a loaf of bread covered with sunflower and sesame seeds. Just as I was thinking that I wanted to have the same thing for lunch, Suzanne came up to me and grabbed my arm.

"I have enough for both of us, so let's go," she said, pulling me toward the meeting room.

The room in the bowels of the health food store was dark, dank and cold. On the periphery was a mismatched assortment of desks, each filled with clutters of paper and food samples left by vendors. Shanta's desk, next to mine, had a large Indian print draped above it for decoration. Across the room was a giant red and black poster of Che Guevara. Underneath the poster was a sloppily cut out quote from Marx: "From each according to his abilities, to each according to his needs."

We dragged our thrift store chairs beneath the light bulb hanging in the middle of the room and started the meeting. Ten of us collectively ran the entire workings of the store. We met weekly. Today we were going to discuss the idea of including developmentally disabled adults in our volunteer program.

I didn't know at the time that this part-time job would turn into a major directional change in my life. But instinctively I knew that this is where I needed to be. It met a deep need to be connected to reality.

I had spent most of my time in laboratories that were devoid of teaming life forms. Everything was in sterile Petri dishes. I understood the rationale: in order to study something, one must begin with a clean palette. When the palette is clean, the scientist can introduce the life form they intend to study.

On my first day of work at Other Avenues, I felt like I was walking into another stream of life. It was clean but far from sterile. On the surface it looked rather funky, especially the meeting room filled with old thrift store chairs and beanbags that had long ago lost their beans.

I was surrounded by wood. Aside from the vegetable coolers, all of the food rested on thick wooden shelving. The honey came in a big five-gallon bucket with a spigot. Customers could fill any size jar they wanted. In the middle of the store were old clunky wooden bins filled with all types of wonderful food. One section was devoted to ten varieties of dried pasta, another to twenty different types of flour.

The air was filled with the aromas of raw honey, cumin, fresh bagels, and coffee. I was dizzy with all the stimulation, but, strangely, I also felt completely at home. This is the world I used to visit with my mother when I was a child. She would cart us two children to tiny basement stores where she always bought wheat germ to put on our cold breakfast cereal. She would also buy bulk oats, coconut, sesame seeds, and pumpkin seeds for batches of homemade granola.

It was within this store with its wonderful aromas that I began to rebuild my cellular structure. Aside from the frequent panic attacks, I had somehow managed to hold myself mostly together through graduate school. In the following years I had devised ways to hide during my panic attacks, hide when the depression swallowed my words, or hide when I couldn't muster the energy to wash my hair.

But now, for the first time, all my actions were visible and transparent. Along with my nine co-owners, I was fully responsible for every aspect of the store. Every year we would review our peers' work. We took this process very seriously, and I witnessed several people lose their jobs during this process.

There was an ethic to be an honest, good, and engaged owner. The entire culture of the store was one of trust and respect for everyone. Workers were paid a real living wage, the food sold was good for the land, and staples like bread, milk, and eggs were sold at cost.

My first year at the store was rough. I hadn't learned how to live from my heart, and I was preoccupied with making things appear right, even when my approach was wrong.

Every week we met to discuss business matters. The group had to agree 100% on everything. Some issues were very serious, like the hiring and firing of collective members. Other issues were more trivial, like whether or not to sell chocolate.

"Marn, pass the strawberry jam. I need some more on my cheese," whispered Suzanne, as we sat listening to one of our co-workers.

I passed it back to her, smiling to myself. I was glad to find a friend who loved food as much as I used to. *Maybe food will be the portal to enjoying life again,* I thought to myself.

After the meeting Suzanne and I walked two blocks north into Golden Gate Park. The leaves were changing to a golden yellow. We both wore scarves around our necks to keep out the crisp air. Like a pair of song birds, our words took flight as we went deeper and deeper into the park's interior. We passed under the towering cypress and Monterey pines, sensing their presence but totally engrossed in conversation.

CHAPTER 27

It was just before dawn. I was lying alone in my bed, dreaming of stocking shelves at Other Avenues, when my mother's hand took mine. It's a touch you can never forget, so familiar and comforting.

Her thumb. Yes, that was her thumb. Her funny, big, flat thumb.

My eyes flew open. Her touch was so real. I stared into my dark narrow room, trying to figure out what reality I was in. My nerves were telling me that the sensation was real, but my rational brain knew that Beverly no longer existed. She had died three years ago. I looked deep into my messy closet, my eyes stopping on the leather jacket my mother bought me years ago.

Now I knew what time stream I was in. I sat up in bed and threw on the sweatshirt that had stayed on the bed with me. I drew in a deep, slow breath and gave voice to my thoughts. *She's dead. She's not in this room with me. But something very real just connected me to her.* I exhaled and let the idea be.

The touch made me miss her but gave me the joy of knowing that she could still convey her love. I got up and put on a pair of Levi's. With effort I pulled open my door and walked into the long hallway toward the kitchen. Liz was sitting at the sun-soaked kitchen table.

"Morning, Liz," I said, letting the love I felt for my mom warm my words.

"Hey, Marn, there's an extra roll on the counter if you want it," Liz said, with her usual generosity.

I grabbed the roll and a wedge of cheese and sat down next to her. I didn't want to share the wonder of what had just happened. Instead I stored it in my sensory experience so I could explore it privately later.

"Are you taking off for the weekend?" she asked.

"Yeah, I'm heading up to Mendocino to stay with Suzanne and Jeff. It's been months since I've seen her. Then I'm back to work on Monday. What are your plans?"

"I'm heading down to Davenport to a manager's meeting. I might just get that promotion," she replied, looking at me with her Scorpio determination.

I knew she would get the job. I smiled at her as I took my last bite.

"See you Monday." I gave her a loving pat on the back and walked down the hallway to my room.

Jeff and Suzanne had grown tired of the city life. Suzanne announced to the collective that she was ready to move on. She was ready to begin living more simply from the land. The town of Willits was perfect for them.

The journey to Suzanne's would be a good three hours. As I got in my car, I looked at my cassette tapes and paused. Better to do without music this morning. I wanted a clear mind to think about what the dawn had brought me.

As the rolling oak woodlands gave way to the mystery of the dark redwoods, I felt my longing for my mother seep into the landscape. It wasn't that long ago that she and I had played in this forest. We pretended that we were witches living among these wise, gentle giants. Now I could feel the spongy space they created. It absorbed and cushioned my sadness and longing, turning my sorrow into celebration.

Suzanne was waiting inside their cozy cabin when I arrived. Jeff, always the active craftsman, was out in the mist gathering firewood. We embraced for a long time, silently acknowledging how much we had missed each other.

She had a pot of soup for lunch simmering on the stove. It was made from root vegetables she had dug from their bountiful garden the day before. Jeff and Sue were deeply committed to living simply and graciously. Their reverence for nature bound them as tightly as their love for each other. Suzanne loved to explore every aspect of the natural world. Jeff devoted himself to mastering it. The room I was standing in was decorated in tables, chests, and bookcases that Jeff had made using Japanese joinery.

"Want a cup of coffee, cutie? I'm trying to quit but I'll have one with you. I picked it up at the co-op. It's organic and roasted in Mendocino," Suzanne said with uncorked excitement.

"Sure. I'd love another cup. I had one at Spinnelli's on my way out."

"So I thought we'd work in the garden until dinner and then come in and work on canning. How does that sound?"

"Great!" I replied, with complete submission. I needed an infusion of Suzanne's energy to draw me out of my heady world and occupy my mind with other things besides why we live and die. Suzanne was all about doing. Today she was making soup, making coffee, knitting a sweater, tanning a hide, and canning tomatoes. She was just the right medicine for a depressive like me.

After lunch we went out to work in the garden. The garden lay across the driveway from the cabin. Jeff had constructed a beautiful wooden gate to welcome people into this verdant space. Suzanne entered before me and immediately began talking to the beets, brushing her hands over the carrot tops, and acknowledging the lettuce with a smile. The vegetables were beautiful, and I could almost feel their companionship. I watched her let the garden absorb her attention. She reminded me of my mother when she entered her art studio to create.

I sat next to her and felt the sponginess of the soil. The carrot bed was full of succulent weeds. Suzanne effortlessly moved her fingers between the carrots' airy leaves to pluck the weeds' round, full leaves and stroke the soil back into place. I could tell by her smooth gestures that her mind was in the moment. We worked wordlessly for awhile.

She stopped weeding and looked up at me. "So how is your meditation practice these days?"

"It's really difficult," I answered. "About the hardest thing I've ever done. Sitting for an hour listening only to my mind can feel like torture. But I did have a breakthrough a couple of months ago."

"Yeah?" Suzanne sat back on her ankles and waited for me to say more.

"I felt, with every cell in my body, a deep and profound connection to everything around me. It was all moving at the same beat. I don't know what it was, but my Taoist teacher said that it may have been a sense of the Tao. Did you ever experience anything like this at Green Gulch?"

Suzanne looked into the distance, and I could tell that she was thinking back to the time when she and Jeff worked at Green Gulch, a Zen Buddhist monastery in the Marin Headlands. She had worked as a volunteer in the gardens, learning the art of mindfulness.

"No. I found a certain peace in my mind but never what you describe. What a gift you were given." She was looking at me intently.

A gift? It feels like a mystery. But I let her words sink in as I looked past a beautiful alder to the moist, sleepy pasture below their house. The light was dripping brownish yellow, touching every blade of grass.

"I don't know what to do with the experience, except to just let it be, and hopefully I'll understand it later in my life," I said, not fully trusting that I could let it be but knowing that I should try.

Something startled me, and I looked down at my hand still in the soil. A worm was making its way across my thumb. Its touch brought me back to our task. We both started weeding again in silence, listening to the sounds of the day.

Slowly my mind began processing. *Touch is a wondrous sensation*, I thought to myself. *It lets you know that you're separate from the world and connected at the same time.*

Suzanne jumped up, landing on her heavy leather boots. "Come on, Marn, we need to start making dinner. It's getting dark."

To my amazement, we had been outside fussing in the soil for over three hours, chatting about life and admiring the carrots and beets. I stood up to follow Suzanne into the cabin, feeling more solid than when I had arrived. I took in the sound of the jay squawking at us as we walked across the red clay driveway. Off in the distance the trees rustled in the gentle breeze.

We walked side by side as we climbed the three stairs to her cabin. I sat on the porch to take off my shoes while Suzanne sat on a beautifully crafted stool Jeff had made. The door gave its squeaky welcome as we entered. Suzanne rushed to the stove to check on some bubbling concoction while I stood in the doorway.

"Marn, are you ok? Why are you standing there?"

"It's so dark in here, I can't see. Can you?"

"Sure, it's just dim."

"Hmm. I've noticed lately that it takes a while for my eyes to adjust and then I'm fine."

Jeff called out my name and gave me a big hug. He was a quiet and reserved man but generous with his affection if you were his friend. We sat by the stove while he began to make a fire. Immediately we dove into a conversation about his Japanese brush painting class. I leaned back on a stack of pillows and let my body relax in the company of these dear friends.

After dinner the three of us sat talking at the table. We had so much to share that we didn't take the time to clear the dishes or turn the Miles Davis record over. Finally, as the moon was high in the sky, we gave in to our fatigue. The lovebirds climbed up into the loft, and I nestled on the futon by the warm woodstove.

Morning came with the jay rustling in the pine. I opened my eyes and sat up to put on my clothes. "Come on, sleepy birds. Time to get up," I called upstairs. I didn't have much time before I needed to make my way back to the city. I put three servings of coffee on the stove.

Driving home I felt renewed by my loving friends. I could feel my heart begin to mend, to being to muster up the courage to move on, despite my mother's death. As I saw the rainbow painted on the Sausalito tunnel behind me and the Golden Gate Bridge ahead, I had an overwhelming sense of what direction my life needed to take. I wanted to start giving back to nature. To touch her soil. I wanted to tend to her and make her well.

CHAPTER 28

On the other side of the Golden Gate lies the Presidio. This old military base and even older Spanish fort was in the process of becoming a National Park. Returning from Suzanne's that morning, I looked out of my car window at the cyprus trees in the newly formed park. My eyes found purpose in these groves of evergreens and rolling dunes.

A few days later I had volunteered to help restore the Presidio, joining the hundreds of volunteers who were pouring their love and creativity into transforming and healing this small corner of the planet. The land had turned poisonous from decades of military abuse. Now park officials imagined the airfield at the historic Crissy Field removed and the sand dunes, estuary, and sea life restored to their original glory.

One of our tasks was to remove the plants that were not native to the landscape. Every Saturday we filled dumpsters with ice plant, scotch broom, pampas grass, and crabgrass brought from other parts of the world to tame the wandering sand dunes. Root by root these plants were being removed to liberate the sand and let the native species thrive again in their shifting soils.

We also collected seeds from the native plants, such as lessengia, coastal buckwheat, seaside daisy, lupine, and sticky monkey flower. The seeds were germinated in the park's native plant nursery and would create a new color palette for the old airstrip, the overgrown Lobos creek, and the Baker Beach sand dunes.

Projects like this were happening all over the Presidio. What was once a military base was now a giant laboratory of restoration. People came from all over to lend their hands and hearts.

I was blessed to be part of it.

*   *   *

Monica, a park intern, walked me to her restoration area. She took a small magnifying glass and held it up against the flower of a lupine.

"This plant is in the pea family; you can see it here in the flower."

I held the magnifier close and looked out over a small, gentle flower. The flower formed a bowl. It was filled with contours, misty pollen, and juicy chambers. A micro creek flowed among the silvery leaves.

We spent 20 minutes looking at this miniature world. I had spent my life enjoying the natural world around me, but I had never cared to stop and really examine this world. My understanding of plants came from textbooks and plastic models of xylem and phloem cells. This was a new world to me.

Our conversation eventually drifted back to the task at hand. We were there to remove the non-native plants that were competing with the native flora. Slowly and diligently, volunteers like Monica and I were tending to the needs of this neglected land.

Slowly, like a gathering tide, I fell deeply and madly in love with this place. I daydreamed about Lobos Creek and drew mental sketches of the dunes above Baker Beach. Every morning as I woke, the beauty of her contours would fill my mind.

I became the steward of a three-acre plot of land west of the old veterans' hospital. It was in a quiet area of the park, far away from the hustle of Baker Beach, Fort Point, and Crissy Field. The plot had been sectioned off as a restoration site because of the delicate, endangered California native plants that clung to a precarious life there. My task involved cataloging the plants, removing the more aggressive non-native plants, replanting baby native plants, and collecting the native plant seeds.

The lizard tail, coastal buckwheat, lessengia, and coyote bush soon became my close friends. I would jump on the 28 bus after a long day at Other Avenues and travel from the sunset district to the Presidio to say hello to them. I would always climb the steep hill inside the plot. It was an acre of vegetated sand dunes. I would sit in the saddle to shield me from the wind while I thought out what task to attempt. I worked until dusk four days a week. My feelings and understanding toward this small spot on the earth grew deeper each week.

Sometimes, in the stillness of the coastal fog, I would sit cross-legged with my back toward the cyprus grove. Using the Taoist meditation techniques I had learned, I would experiment with holding my mind in stillness so that I could sense the delicate signature of this little place. I began to notice the pattern the winds always took, what leaves always shook, where the flowers bloomed, and the quality of the sound waves.

For the first time in my life I realized that nature and I could dance together. She was willing to give herself to me. And in exchange I would tend to her.

I would restore her. Heal her.

CHAPTER 29

Every week our health food store accumulated heaps of vegetable waste from our produce display. The trimmings would rot away in large garbage bins, waiting to be hauled away for landfill. It bothered me.

Somewhere along my walks in San Francisco I remembered seeing a large, rectangular bin that had three chambers in it. It was a composting bin for food scraps. I decided that we should build our own. With the help of my fellow collective members, we soon had our first composting bin in the store's backyard where we composted vegetable scraps and wood chips. It was the start of an exciting journey.

My curiosity soon outgrew the small yard, and I approached my friends in the Presidio about building large, open piles in the park. Soon we had giant, steaming loaves of bread. I liked to think that they helped create the fog that lingered high over the Golden Gate Bridge.

"Hey! Can you move the truck a bit closer to the dumpster?" I had to shout at my friend Damien over the wind.

"I'll try, but I'm not used to driving such a big truck," he yelled back with his kind, helpful voice.

I was standing knee deep in a 20-yard dumpster full of horse manure and bedding. The ammonia was so thick that at times it took my breath away.

Every Saturday Damien and I would meet at the horse stables in an abandoned part of the Presidio to build our luscious compost "cakes." We would run around in an old Ford, forking in various ingredients for our piles. At one stop we would drive up to the backside of the prestigious golf course and load up the grass clippings from the day, the smell hitting me like an immediate anti-depressant. Our next stop was the pile of woodchips that was nearly as tall as the three-story veterans' hospital that it was next to.

This part of the old military base was an eerie combination of abandoned 1950's style buildings and vibrant, rare dune wildflowers. It was almost always foggy here, and the wind would whip the tall cypress trees around like seaweed in a turbulent ocean. Occasionally the fog would lift enough so that we could see the landscape around us. The dune flowers appeared delicate and shy, but they were strong enough to survive the rugged conditions.

Among the wildflowers and across the old cement bridge was a graveyard full of unnamed merchant marines. Their graves were nearly hidden among the blooming lizard tail, seaside daisy, and coastal buckwheat. It was here in this blooming graveyard that we filled our truck with chipped pine and cypress. This was the carbon source for our compost piles.

It was ten o'clock in the morning, and we had already gathered one truckload of horse manure that was unloaded at the native plant nursery and one truck-load of grass clippings from the golf course. We were now on our second load of wood chips from the foggy graveyard.

Damien's energy was fading. He had a bad habit of skipping breakfast, and by this time he was usually toast. Luckily I knew this about him and always had a stash of bread with peanut butter in the truck. A rich protein source always brought him back to life, which was a good thing because the best part of our day was about to begin.

Adjacent to the native plant nursery was a small, abandoned lot that was assigned to me to use as my composting laboratory. It was here that Damien and I would deposit our piles of debris. Here on this foggy spot, a thousand yards from the Golden Gate Bridge, I began my journey back to the world of the living. Back to the days when I was a kid exploring the woods with my 5th grade science class.

I had come back to the natural world via an unusual guide. It may seem odd to use the process of decay as a point of departure for my rebirthing journey. But she couldn't have been a more perfect teacher.

When I first gathered these "dead" ingredients to make my compost piles, I wasn't prepared for the incredibly beautiful transformation that would take place. In just four months, the old wood chips, stinky grass clippings, and foul horse manure would reorganize themselves into a rich, loamy, luscious medium that was teeming with microbial life.

Eventually I began making compost on a grand scale. In two years I was hired full-time by the Presidio Trust and was making enough compost to provide a growing medium for the native plant nursery. These plants, after many years of love and care from hundreds of volunteers, regenerated an old airfield back to its original glory—a coastal marshland.

The journey was deeply healing to my soul.

I wasn't able to save my mother's life, but I played a part in regenerating our relationship to a larger "mother."

I loved making compost. It was my sanctuary. Every day I would arrive at work and bury myself in the death and rebirth cycle. It slowly began to lift my heavy darkness. The decomposition process was so complex, yet so mundane. It was a puzzle intellectually, and I would spend many sleepless nights trying to try figure out how these molecules could reorganize themselves into humus. Other times I would meditate on the metaphoric quality of the process.

A vibrant, green grass clipping could change into a dry, brown clipping in 24 hours. Where did the green go? Why does the composting process move chromatically from bright greens, reds, and oranges to light browns and eventually to a dark chocolate brown? The color of the browns in the middle of the process always seems lackluster, but the brown that emerges after the reorganization of molecules happens is practically luminescent.

It was through the delicately delicious browns of the compost that I found the desire to experience color again. But I needed a guide. As luck would have it, I found the perfect teacher in Ryan, a young, enthusiastic watercolor painter.

Ryan had started as a volunteer at the Presidio, but his talent in painting landed him a job painting watercolors of the park's flora and fauna. I had met him two years before in the lobby of the park stewards building. He was drawing pelicans and butterflies on the white cinder block wall. These larger-than-life images were the beginnings of a mural. He filled the room with his infectious enthusiasm.

Ryan was a beautiful young man. He was only seventeen, but he had a timeless soul and an open, welcoming heart. I found his soft nature sexy. Ryan's body radiated the same light that he displayed in his paintings, and it invited flirtation.

The light that emerged from his watercolors drew me in. I knew that my eyes, sore from sobbing, needed to learn to dance with the light again. One day I mustered up the nerve to ask if he would teach me the art of watercolor. He said yes without hesitation.

I rode my Diamond Back mountain bike along the single-track trails to get to Ryan's apartment. He lived in the old army barracks in the Presidio, a series of ugly, rectangular buildings nestled in the sand dunes across from Baker Beach.

"Hey, come on in. I have everything ready for our lesson," Ryan greeted me, with his usual enthusiasm.

His living room was warm and well lit. The back wall was concealed by a layer of records. I dropped my coat and went straight for the LP's I recognized.

"Wow, Fats Waller! Fantastic!" I exclaimed.

"Yeah, we can play it when we take a break," Ryan said, gently redirecting me.

The lesson began with playing with colors. Under Ryan's instruction, I spent an hour painting red, red, and red on my paper. Then yellow, yellow, and yellow. It was wondrous. Depending on my touch, the color would be bold or subtle. If I took up too much water on the brush, the color was soft. If I was greedy on the pigment, the color was bold.

I chuckled to myself. "I thought painting was about the object, not about the color. This is so much fun."

"Let's take a break," Ryan said, jumping to his feet. He went over to the record player and put on Frank Sinatra. His smooth voice made the colors all around us even lusher. Before I knew it we were dancing. He led and I followed very clumsily. Soon I relaxed and gave in. We started laughing. Spinning and laughing like lovers, but it was platonic and not romantic. Ryan knew my sexual preference and honored it.

After an hour we went back to painting. The soft light warmed the ocean apartment. I felt extremely content and entertained by the colors and how the water brought the pigment to life.

The following week we painted an apple.

I dipped my brush into the paint and made round, full motions. I repeated the motions, this time taking up a bit of black with the red. Next I took up a little yellow and smoothed that color into the mix. It seemed like the colors were marble and I was peeling back the layers to reveal a stone sculpture of an apple. Hidden within this color was the life of an apple. Or so I thought. My apple didn't look like an apple.

"Ryan, this looks terrible!"

"Just give it time; you need to build the relationship between the dark and the light. Keep working the edges with the color."

I had no idea what he was talking about.

He rose from his chair and came over to my sad little apple. In a matter of minutes, the image bloomed before my eyes. By working with the dark shadows and the color, his apple was luminous. The periphery and center danced to make a whole. The apple lifted off the page.

As I rode my bike home after class I stopped to look at the grand Pacific. The blue of the sea danced into my eyes. A tear slid down my cheek. For over a decade I had gazed upon this vast sea, and I had not seen its glory until today. Just like a light illuminating a room, I could perceive colors again.

Exploring color with Ryan had begun to restore my raw, depressed nerves. Once again I began to see the subtle emotions of the natural world around me. The anger within the red Indian paint brush, the cool, sad blue of the lupine, the joyful yellow of the lessengia.

Then, after a few months, my color memory came back. At first just some flashes in the early morning hours. Then I saw the reds of Spain again. I recalled the blues of Southern France and the brown-grays of a New York winter.

I recalled the exact color of my mother's hair.

CHAPTER 30

Grounding myself in the "wilds" of the Presidio, I began to feel connected to myself. With my feet able to feel the warmth of the earth, I felt confident to widen my social circle.

Liz, no longer my roommate but still a good friend, called me on the phone to attend a beach bonfire with her. It was a lesbian social for the Bernal Heights neighborhood. As she and I walked toward the orange campfire from the parking lot, I stood close to her. I knew no one and suddenly felt shy.

"Marney Blair, is that you?" called a familiar voice.

I turned and saw the face of an old friend from graduate school.

"Karen, how the hell are you!" I gave her a big bear hug, then stood back and took a good look at her. *Yup, she's as cute as I remember.*

We chatted and laughed on the beach for the rest of the evening, then traded phone numbers before saying our goodbyes. Clearly, the spark from our graduate school days was still there. Within two weeks we were dating.

We had fun hiking, walking the dogs, listening to music, and eating out in the city's many tasty restaurants. Karen had music salons on the weekends, when she would open up her living room and invite musician friends to play. Karen herself had a wonderful Northern California style on the guitar, earnest like Joan Baez but light and melodic like Bruce Cockburn.

We enjoyed our time together, but both of us knew that we weren't in love.

* * *

It was 3:30 on a warm weekend afternoon. The sunbeams heated the interior of my room as I gingerly climbed into bed. Karen, who had brought me home, walked to the bright windows and drew the curtains.

"Oh, yes. Thanks for doing that," I said, feeling the immense pressure swell in my head.

Karen looked down at me, the concern showing on her face. I looked away, wanting to be alone despite feeling afraid.

"I'll call you tonight to make sure you're OK," she said, kissing my head and gently closing the door behind her.

I let out a long breath and tried desperately to relax every cell in my body. I had been having a fine day running around the city with Karen. We had eaten a late breakfast of dim sum on Geary Street and then walked around in the Richmond neighborhood. Eventually we had made our way back to her car where the pressure in my head began to build. As we drove through Golden Gate Park the nausea was so intense that I felt like I wanted to die.

"Hey, you gotta pull over," I managed to say, holding back surges of acidic fluid. As I heaved in the bushes by the side of the road, I was keenly aware of the bike riders, joggers, and walkers staring at me as they passed by. I was embarrassed. I was really sick.

I stayed there for a few minutes, dry heaving. Then I felt my head clear, and I knew this was my only chance to get in the car and make it home without another bout of nausea. Flashes of light pulsed all around my visual field like a fireworks display. I closed my eyes and tried desperately to stop the internal neural firing.

Back at home, I slept for five hours in the dark silence of my room.

At nine p.m. I walked into the kitchen to find something to eat. I was no longer sick to my stomach, but my entire nervous system felt exhausted and I felt my body vibrating to a strange frequency. I poured a bowl of cold cereal and went back to my bedroom. I didn't want to chat with my roommates.

These periodic spells were a puzzle to me. The migraine-like symptoms, which would come on in a matter of minutes, had become more and more frequent in the past year. I was also finding myself experiencing claustrophobia, usually associated with restaurants, meetings, and large gatherings of people. These were the only clues I had to work from. I turned to friends who were competent in the field of alternative health care. They checked me out and said I was fine and just needed rest. Their assessment was sufficient for me and also served as an excuse not to see a western medical doctor. After all that I had seen, I didn't trust western medicine.

My thoughts shifted as I stared at the night sky from my bedroom window. In two days I would be flying to Denver for a stress-free vacation with my old friend Tawnya. We planned to camp and mountain bike in western Colorado. I wanted to see the town of Ourey again, drive through the San Juans, and eventually ride some trails on some mesas outside of Grand Junction. Compared to other biking trips, this would be an easy trip along a gorge on clearly marked trails.

I had made arrangements to borrow a friend's bike in Boulder. It was equipped with new, more responsive brakes and shifters on the handlebars. Her bike made my old Diamond Back look like a beach cruiser.

Tawnya picked me up at the airport in her familiar beige Toyota pickup. The truck, with a camper shell on the back, was looking its age. She had lived in it for years when she moved to New Mexico from California. When I would visit periodically we would drive the truck out onto a mesa outside of Taos and set up camp for the night. Inside the shell was a comfy mattress, milk crates organized for making coffee or a meal, flashlights, books, beach chairs from her old California days, and toilet paper. Tawnya now lived in a wonderful adobe house, but "Little Truck" was always ready for camping.

Today we were driving over the Continental Divide. As we drove into the sunrise, the thin air filled my lungs and woke up childhood memories. My love for nature began here in these grand Rocky Mountains when I was young. The douglas fir standing tall by the freeway reminded me of summers long gone when my father, brother, and I would go fishing in small alpine lakes. We would spend the day listening to the wind, the jays, and the splash of icy lake water. It felt good to be home. My muscles relaxed into the torn brown seat and I began to sing along with my friend and Joan Armatrading.

I was feeling good. I was with a dear old friend in an old, familiar town. Grounded in this place I gave in to old, familiar feelings of sadness, longing, elation, and bliss. I now felt strong enough to carry such depths of feeling, thanks mostly to my work in the Presidio and friends like Suzanne.

As we drove further and further into the wide band of the Rockies, I felt my emotional body hum in harmony with the picturesque landscape. The craggy cliffs, the alpine meadows, the familiar tunes we sang all made joy surge through my body. Finally I could share the pain of losing my mom with my old friend. It felt good.

We exited the freeway and found a dirt road that led into BLM land. We drove in slowly, looking for any flat turnout area that could serve as a good camping spot. The truck stopped, and I got out to inspect a promising spot.

"This looks perfect," I announced.

"I'll pull in next to that log," Tawnya replied.

"And someone left a pile of wood to burn! We picked a lucky spot."

The night was cold, but we were not. The firewood was dry and burned intensely. After some dinner and beer we climbed into the truck and pulled a heavy down comforter over us. The alpine stars twinkled beyond my eyelids and filled my retinas with star dust as I fell into a gentle, light sleep.

The red soils of Colorado filled the landscape as I looked around the campsite in the morning light. Tawnya sat next to me, drinking coffee and looking at a map of the area we were going to ride that day. The air was still and the newly risen sun drew whatever moisture was in the air. As I sat drinking my strong coffee, I knew by the stillness that it was going to be a warm day. A perfect day for mountain biking.

Once we reached the site, we jumped on our bikes and I started to descend into a canyon area below the primary mesa. The top-of-the-line bike I had borrowed was much more responsive than my old clunker. It took just a slight touch to engage the brakes.

I saw a large rock in the trail ahead of me, signaling that I needed to brake and hop to the left. I did but found myself tumbling into a rock outcrop.

I sat stunned.

I wasn't hurt physically. My ego was bruised. *Darn, I really misread that one. Guess I'm a bit rusty.*

I looked up to see Tawnya jumping and dodging ahead of me. She was graceful and at home on her bike. She glanced back and could see that I was down.

"No worries! I'm just not used to these brakes," I yelled to her.

I picked up the bike, dusted off myself and my self-doubt, and moved quickly down the trial.

Smack.

I sat for a minute trying to assess what had happened. *That was a hard fall, and I never even saw it coming. I guess I'll have to ride more slowly until I get the hang of this bike.* I stood up, feeling a bit shaken. I had been mountain biking for two decades. The thrill of whizzing by scenery and sweating in the thin mountain air always gave me a shot of pure joy.

OK, girl, let's get this right!

I looked ahead and saw the route of the trail before me. It moved down into a narrow area and then hugged the hillside as it wrapped above a deep canyon. The trail made a beautiful line. I hoped that I was ready for the thrill.

Feeling a bit unnerved, I started cautiously. I stopped my bike a couple of times and walked over the tricky areas. When I was riding the curve, I looked down into the vast canyon below. Rocks of a different shade lived down there. I could see a ribbon of water twist its way around the boulders.

Suddenly I was off the trail and swinging my arms through the loose shale, trying to find anything solid to stop my descent. When I found something, I clung to it like a magnet. I was lucky that I hadn't fallen too far into the canyon.

I scrambled up the steep incline and sat down on the trail. I had no idea what was going on with me. I felt that I had adjusted to this new bike; she felt good and under my command. I also thought that I had polished the rust away and had my groove back. But as I sat there, my desire to bike dissolved into the red soil around me.

I stood up and pulled the bike away from its resting place, a thick bunch of sage brush. I wedged it onto my shoulder and walked all the way back to the truck, my body hurt and bleeding. As fellow bikers rode past me, I stood beside the trail with my head down. I didn't want to make eye contact. This was embarrassing.

Back sitting on the tailgate of "Little Truck" I cried big, heavy tears. I couldn't figure out what had gone so wrong. My mind and spirit were as deflated as a punctured balloon.

"Gosh, Marn, are you ok?"

I began to describe to Tawnya what had happened. She gave me a gentle hug. We sat in silence, drinking beer and staring off into the vast Colorado plateau. She was confused, too. We had ridden many miles together for many years. I knew her to be an incredible athlete, and she saw me in the same light. Marney Blair: skier, lacrosse player, track and field runner, backpacker, and avid mountain biker.

As we drove back to our campsite, I made the silent decision that the mishaps were due to the unfamiliar bike and a rusty rider. I had no idea that the problem was inside of me. I didn't know that the darkness was bleeding slowly into my visual field, erasing my ability to perceive the heights of rocks and the depth of grooves in the trail. It was inconceivable to me that my ability to perceive light was slowly fading and leaving me in the dark.

CHAPTER 31

I was perched high above the ground in my tractor in the Presidio. To the west I could make out the movement of the great Pacific. As I turned the tractor around to pick up a load of wood chips, I faced the shuttered Pacific Health Services Hospital. The massive, light brown, brick structure melted into the sandy colors around it. The hospital was silent and eerie. This was the forgotten side of the park, and it made a perfect site for a noisy composting operation.

I swung open the cab door of the 120-horse-power John Deere tractor to hear my assistant's voice.

"I need you to look at this composting windrow! It's not heating properly!" she shouted over the rumble of the tractor's engine.

I jumped down from the seat I had occupied for two hours. My steel-toed boots thumped against the pavement as I walked toward the hundred-foot compost pile we had made two months ago. I dug my hands into the pile and brought the mass to my nose. I felt my spine straighten up. I was confident that I could figure out the problem.

I approached the composting process like a lover. I took books to bed and slept with molecules of organic matter floating around my body. I studied the aromas of compost and the changing colors of her matter. Its mysteries and organic beauty attracted me intellectually and emotionally. I was grateful to have such a wonderful lover.

"The carbon to nitrogen ratio is off," I told my assistant. "Maybe the grass clippings are older than I thought. Take the temperature of all the raw materials and we can start from there." I glanced at my watch. "I have to meet someone at the Golden Gate Bridge in ten minutes, so let's talk again later this afternoon."

I drove off in my electric Ford Ranger to meet a woman named Lisa and her sister. They wanted to tour the facility. We had planned the meeting weeks in advance. Lisa had gotten my phone number from my friend Karen and called me one Sunday morning. Karen thought that Lisa and I should get to know each other since we both enjoyed working outdoors. Lisa and her sister were visiting their mother in Marin and were curious to see what a large-scale composting facility looked like. I was excited about the meeting but wasn't sure why.

I was facing Golden Gate Bridge when Lisa walked around the truck and into my view. Both the wind and time seemed to stop as I gazed upon the most luminescent, earthy person I had ever seen. Her arms and legs swung with seductive confidence as her lanky frame approached me. She was vibrating with energy. I didn't notice what she was wearing because I was so drawn to her face. As we shook hands, I looked into her welcoming eyes. I could tell immediately from her smile and the light from her eyes that she was an open, loving person.

Her older sister had more delicate features and laughed at my silly jokes as we walked to my truck. I drove to the compost yard feeling distracted and slightly giddy.

I was always proud to show off my composting operation. I was finally in a place in my life where I felt rooted and nourished by the earth. As I opened the gate to my yard, I felt the strength of my own stride. I had spent countless hours walking the trails of this land, collecting her seeds, sowing her plants, and nourishing her with my compost. In return, these sandy dunes had anchored me and given me structure.

I was ready to live again.

I was already madly in love. I loved San Francisco, and I dearly loved this piece of land. My first glance of this light-filled woman was stunning. I knew her; she had been with me all along in my imagination. Now she was here, and I was ready to be swept into the winds of another kind of love.

CHAPTER 32

After three hours of driving, I turned off Highway 49
onto a narrow, one-lane private road. The sandy dunes
of San Francisco felt far away as I entered the community of Sierra Silver Pine. The soil was an iron red and the
undulating road lined with large boulders, manzanita
bushes, and silver pine heavy with pine cones. Soon the
road began to descend, crossing a creek and leveling out
in a long, narrow meadow. Off in the distance I could
see a structure that looked like a barn. This was the
house that Lisa had built with her own hands. It looked
just as she had described it on the phone.

The plan was to spend the day together on her
land. How glorious it would be to see her bright smile
again. This would be our first date alone. My stomach
was knotted with anticipation.

I pulled my white 1989 Subaru wagon into the
dusty driveway and walked toward the pond. We had
decided to meet in her garden. As I rounded the corner
of a majestic valley oak, I saw her strong body working
the soil. I stopped and watched her rhythm as she took
up heavy clods of dirt with her fork and placed them
back on the garden bed, each time turning the fork on
its side to strike the clod and loosen the heavy clay dirt.
She was completely immersed in the activity.

I knew at this moment that we would be starting an incredible journey together. I knew by looking at her strong, bare shoulders tanning in the sun that we would create magic together. The strength of her arms would complement my strong, dense thighs. Her warm, dark Italian skin would blend with my pink-white hide.

I walked toward her with all the confidence in the world. I knew that I would give myself completely. I was ready for this incredible adventure.

For the next year, weekends were the time for weaving our lives together. Every other week Lisa would load her two dogs into the truck and stay two days at my foggy place in San Francisco. Our urban adventures centered around eating, hiking, mushroom hunting on Mount Tamalpais, visiting family, and "book storing." Alternate weekends I would load up my Subaru and drive three hours to spend time working in her garden, visiting her friends, hiking, cooking, and stargazing.

My heart surprised me. After decades of pain, I wasn't sure that she could beat vibrant red blood through my body. Now my swollen heart moved fluid full of life and light all around my newly sensuous body. As I moved around in this new world, sparks of light danced off of my skin. Sometimes the light would jump free and illuminate another person nearby. I was electric.

After four seasons we were ready to bring our lives together forever. The land that was so special to her was calling me, too, so I resigned from my Presidio job. I was sad to leave such a family of friends. The community of wildflowers had filled my days with joy. I had worked so hard to build up a successful composting operation, and now I was willing to let it go. Because I knew that this love for Lisa was the real thing.

I believe that love between people creates a third being. In our case, this being was the "DNA" to create a farm. So this is what we set out to do. Within a year both of us were turning over the soil in the Sierra Foothills.

The farm grew over the years from our daily imaginations of how the animals would move, how the water would travel, how the tractor would harvest, and how the deer could still move to the creek to drink. Some of the fences held a straight line. Other fences took on the contour of the land.

Joy poured from our work as we moved images from our minds to the landscape. We were growing an integrated farm organism. Each of us had our role. The dogs chased the raccoons. The chickens ate the beetles and the worms from the cow patties. The turkeys ate the culled seeds. The pigs ate the whey from the cheese making. The corn and beans ate the compost from the pig, chicken, turkey, and cow manure. The cows ate the abundant spring grass. The cats ate the mice. The farmers ate it all.

Dreamy ideas began to turn into solid plans. Take the chicken coop. It began with a whimsical idea: to use an old camper as a shelter for hens.

I drove our small tractor down a modest slope and stopped in front of the brown and silver 1960s camper shell. We tied a strap around it and tried to lift it from its resting place.

It didn't budge.

We sat in the soft spring grass and stared at the heavy hunk of metal.

"This camper shell is way heavier than I thought," Lisa announced.

"It feels like it's stuck to the ground!" I added, half joking.

"The tractor should be able to lift it," Lisa said, as we continued to stare at the inert lump. She jumped up. "I got it! The angle is all wrong on the tractor arm!"

I jumped up too and started loosening the strap from the shell. Soon we began working as one, both of us able to see in our creative minds the correct way to lift the darn thing. Eventually we had the strap repositioned in such a way that the hydraulics on the tractor should be able to wrestle the camper from its earthly anchor. I got up on the tractor, excited and confident. Slowly and with lots of creaking, the big object let go of the earth. I raised it into the air, my eyes glued to Lisa's body moving around the camper to check the state of the strap. Her hand raised in a gesture to stop. Then, with a confident ok, she motioned me to drive forward.

Like ants moving an object twenty times their size, we lumbered slowly down the field, precariously carrying the old camper shell toward the pond. A final loud creak and squeak and the camper flattened the grass in its new spot. I jumped off the tractor and into Lisa's outstretched arms with such excitement that we fell to the ground. We rolled around the lush green pasture, soaking up the gold light of our love. Eventually we rolled apart and, holding hands, gazed up at the cloudless sky.

As if the concept came from the dreamy heavens, we began to articulate what the new chicken coop would be. We would make art. The chickens would be laying their eggs in a giant, brown egg.

And so they did. For the top of the giant egg, we used rebar wrapped together to make a soft point. Then we used metal lath to make a skeleton over the entire shell. We covered the lath with light brown stucco. Finally we added the laying boxes and three rows of roosts. It was whimsical, yet functional.

The hens loved it.

CHAPTER 33

The alluring fragrance from the rose draws me to the corner of the garden that I've been avoiding. This is the corner where I buried Sophie's calf seven months earlier, the calf named after my mother. In the past I always circled wide to smell the beautiful pink roses. But now the sweet smell seems to tell me that I have nothing to fear.

As I stand over the grave I realize how much stronger I've become. I feel myself standing tall and let the lovely fragrance move in and out of my nose. Time has allowed the calf beneath this soil to decay and transform, just as it has given me the freedom to embrace life's harshness. The soil, the rose, the grass that grows above her grave, and the music from the babbling creek are all my companions on this journey.

I hear the rumble of the tractor close by. The sound brings me to the task at hand.

Today we are working an acre, supporting the soil so that it can be a fertile womb to carry the seeds. The spring air is electric. The spader hovers above the soil as it churns and methodically breaks up the soil. The aroma is more satisfying to me than the first sniff of a fine merlot.

As Lisa drives the orange tractor slowly through the field, I follow behind, raking spots in the soft, spongy soil that are too delicate for the tractor. This is our springtime dance with the earth. Lisa moves slowly forward and I move perpendicularly to her line. Together we're making a luscious, open soil bed.

Three hours later, we have half an acre ready for planting. It is a rich, blank canvas waiting to be filled. The seeds will become plants that grow tall, spread thickly on the ground, or stand in tight bunches. The moment the young plants break the soil's crust, the insects will appear. They'll fly and crawl. They'll bring shimmering colors and sounds. Eventually the field will be dotted with light-filled flowers and the air filled with the constant movement of pollen and insects.

After a lunch of corn tortillas, beans, cabbage, and cheese, we're ready to bring the seed and soil together. Taking a sweet, dense seed in my hand, I use my thumb and forefinger to gently press her into the earth. I'll plant thousands of seeds this way. Each time the gesture feels deep and satisfying. When I finish each row, I stand up and look back at it, imagining what my eyes will behold in a week. I could use a mechanical seeder, but I'm addicted to the sensory experience of pushing the seed through the earth's diaphragm. Each time I press past the springy, imaginary membrane I feel a connection with this primal birthing process.

After planting the field we'll move to fence building. Like putting paint on canvas, the line of the fence will define space. It will create an in and out, volume and depth, horizontal and vertical, and pasture and untamed land.

The work of digging, shoveling, tamping the dirt, and carrying the wood brings song and laughter to our voices. We are two farmers dancing with a muse that allows us to see where the fence must bend and curve.

"Let's have the fence move gracefully around the apricot tree," Lisa says, sharing her vision.

I ponder this image for a moment. "What a beautiful idea. It'll make a wonderful area to have lunch and watch the cows graze," I reply, imagining a picnic of home-grown tomato, basil, and onion salad.

Within a week, the wooden fence is done. We stand back and admire our work. The space is defined. With a simple line on the earth we've created a beautiful space for the home, the picnic, and the pasture. We've created a boundary that will serve as energetic meeting places, like the energy created by a cell wall, a creek bed, the spot where meadow and woods meet, or the touch between lovers.

It is the synergy of our artistic sensibilities that is giving shape to this space. I dig deep inside myself and listen to the words of my mother. Lisa uses her artistic eye to find the balance. Together we're beginning to create a place that will harmonize with nature.

This miracle lives peacefully in my mind. It has the same quality as the love that I have been blessed with. The vibration from this love between us makes me feel bold and courageous. I am beginning to get a deep sense of healing the earth, as I had with my work in the Presidio. But now this force of love is catapulting me into larger realms. I want to halt the polluting of our earth mother and all the plant and animal mothers. I want to immerse myself deeply into the art of farming, to grow food that will nourish humans. I am ready to dive into healing humans. Perhaps even myself.

I can sense my mother's spirit swelling with joy as Lisa and I begin a life of service. Her voice reminds me of the need for beauty, symmetry, and color. Now I can live within her memory.

CHAPTER 34

The way the eye works is beautiful and complex. A tiny package of light enters the eye and travels through a watery solution to the back of the eye, known as the retina. There it travels through eight layers of cells before it strikes a rod or cone cell. These cells are designed to convert light energy to chemical energy. So the light particle travels through the entire structure of the eye before it ever illuminates--before it can release its energy.

Rhodopsin is a special protein that absorbs the energy of the light and creates a cascade of ion gradients. This cascade is an internal wind of sorts and moves the chemical impulse, which at this moment becomes a nerve impulse, to the visual cortex in the brain.

In the brain a very interesting thing happens. The brain perceives light by comparing the relative light and dark regions of the retina. In effect it reads a map of the retina and compares areas with and without the packets of energy. Light actually inhibits the signaling of the rod and cone cells, so more light particles signal a darker response. In other words, we see based on a complex relationship between light and dark.

*   *   *

"The Supreme Court will hear arguments on the Affordable Health Care Act today...." My coffee percolates while I listen to the day's news on the radio near my kitchen stove. I carefully pour the black stimulant into my ceramic mug, the black swirling in a counter clockwise motion as it mixes with Rosa's cream.

"It is going to be a decision that will affect millions...."

I turn off the radio and walk out the front door. The earthy spring air massages my face, and my worries over the national news take flight with the breeze. I draw a deep, satisfied breath. The day is all mine.

The air is still cool, but the exuberant song of the house finch warms me. My head bobs in rhythm as he sings his tune again and again. This sweet sound of spring is broken by a demanding bark. Mo, our farm dog, is complaining that she hasn't gotten her breakfast. Her inflection demands my full attention, and I quickly poor some kibble in the dog bowls.

I watch Mo and her companion Sydney as they inhale their food. The early morning light carries the warmth of Mo's golden coat to my eyes. The gold color is familiar, but it's the warmth within the gold that is the clue to her vitality.

Good. She seems to be doing very well.

My eyes move to Sydney's black coat. Her luster appears even more vibrant. Perhaps it is her youth that I'm seeing. She's young compared to Mo, who is now nearing the equivalent of eighty human years.

I shift my attention away from the crunching and licking and back to the sounds of the house finch. He's still moving through his signature repertoire. The song of songbirds always fills a deep place in my chest.

The vibration moves down and into an ancient part of my cells. The familiar springtime songs seem to echo in some deep cosmic core within me.

They awaken my Persephone. Spring is here.

I walk out to the pasture to greet the cows, my companion Sydney skipping delightedly behind me. The finch's song is replaced by the delicate thump of hooves striking the dense clay soil. The earthy sound puts weight on my feet, and my body suddenly feels manifest. I climb the fence and drop into the cows' corral, my feet meeting the ground with purpose.

A worn piece of pine keeps the door shut on the small hay barn. My hand feels the smooth finish created by years of oily human hands. It feels just right as I lift it into the air for the ten thousandth time. Inside are heavy bales of last summer's growth. I slide my knife over the bailing twine, and the unbound grass springs to life. As I peel back a flake of hay, the sweet aroma makes me salivate.

Good enough for the girls to eat, I say out loud to whomever may be listening. I place a flake in front of each cow. As usual, I pause for a moment, listening to their sounds of chewing, breathing, and moving.

I stretch my arms out to find the fence and hoist my body onto the rail. As I jump to the other side, my neighbors' car whizzes past. The velocity startles me, and I jump back toward the fence. I hadn't seen it coming. I quickly wave a greeting. No response. I wonder what their morning has been like. Did they take the time to hear the house finch sing?

This place in time, the *now* time, feels best on my nerves. When my senses are grounded in real time, ear, nose, eye and skin stimulation allows me to run on reflexes. I have a different sense of myself when my attention moves inward. Then I get caught up in a process of distilling what I sense, and though these thoughts are often beguiling, they take me away from the world unfolding around me.

"You are blind. It would be best to look into a seeing eye dog." I repeat this statement from the retinal specialist out loud.

Darkness. I will live in total darkness.

The light will move into my eyes, but I will not be able to perceive its presence. The light energy is wasted, bouncing around in the eye with no cells to receive it.

I will be all alone.

This must be why he suggested a dog. Yes, the dog will be my only true companion for she will digest the light for me. The dog will be an extension of my eyes. The dog will connect me to the world.

I sit under a grand blue oak tree. I'm stiff from the cold. I feel the old bark crunch against my spine.

This is my fate.

The dog will be a nice companion. But my god, I will be alone. I will be left to create a world only from my brain's distillations. I will never again have a direct visual experience of my world. The dead retinal cells feel dead. I have no experience of light from the outer circle of my eyes. Blank. It is dark. I am dark. I can see nothing.

Suddenly Sydney is in my face, dropping a ball for me to throw. Our eyes meet.

"Come on, throw it," her eyes say. I toss the ball into the green pasture. She dashes after it with springtime vigor. My mind shifts from my dark thoughts to the smooth nature of Sydney's chasing instincts. I draw in a deep breath, taking in the smells of enlivened dirt. I take another and cherish the sensation of the air moving into my blood.

Sydney's tail is wagging, telling me that she's ready for another chase. I look into her eyes. *I will be all right. I will not be alone.*

I walk out to the area below our house. On the picnic table are cedar boxes filled with compost and dirt. My hand reaches for the soft, inviting soil. My fingers dive in and around the moist pockets of life.

"Hey, I want to plant those San Marzanos again this year. They're fantastic for the CSA. Everyone loves dried tomatoes," I say to Lisa, while looking for the seed packet.

"Yeah, they're great. Let's plant some Kimberton Yellow too. I just planted the Chadwich Cherries." Lisa's enthusiasm is infectious.

"Yummy. This is gonna be a good growing year. I can feel it."

I look up from the dark soil into the woods beyond the creek. The trees glow with green optimism. I
let the spring light lift my spirits.

CHAPTER 35

The sun has settled on an arc today that makes the shadows longer and deeper. I've noticed the changes that come with fall: the gradual decline of available sunlight, the light dampening like the moist air moving down the hillside behind the creek, the colors cooler and richer as they bounce off the pasture. I feel a tightening in my neck from the strain that I unconsciously place on my eyes.

As I walk into the pasture to bring the sleepy cows around, I step into a hole and tumble to the ground. I saw this hole during the summer months when the green plantain and clover in its depression became darker green and eventually black. I have trained my eye to watch for such contrasts. But the sun's angle makes it harder to judge the depth of the depressions.

The fall equinox is almost here. I have to adjust my perception. Slow down my pace, I say to myself as I push off from the dark soil beneath my hand. I must prepare myself emotionally for the dark days ahead. Once I've accepted the reality of shorter days, I can begin to feel the restorative quality that darkness has on my eyes.

I follow behind the cows as they walk into the corral. Lisa puts each cow in her stanchion. They're ready for their morning milking. My hand stretches out to feel the worn, oiled wooden handle as I latch the gate. I reach for the cow's hind quarter. I feel her warmth and solid presence. My hand on her centers me visually. Although I cannot see her entire body, I can feel that she is steady and calm.

I milk this cow twice a day. We share an intimacy. Her tail swats the back of my head if I become preoccupied with human worries. The gesture brings me back to the present, reminds me to breathe and focus on removing the milk from her udder. It is a rejuvenating, milking meditation.

Eventually my morning chores are done. I can now feed myself, go over the day's schedule with Lisa, and rest my eyes a bit.

I walk into the kitchen, eager for a hot cup of coffee. The dim light is making the kitchen look heavy and cavernous, and every object appears muted. It catches me off guard. I hear the front door close and feel Lisa coming into the kitchen. She moves with the ease and determination of a squirrel rushing to collect acorns for winter. She's ready for her caffeine, too. The kitchen dance begins.

Panic hits me. I cannot see well enough to manage while both of us are making breakfast. It's too much information for my brain to process. I try to slowly remove a plate from the shelf. I back up into Lisa, and we both whisper "sorry." I lean into the cabinet and let the fear and frustration wash over me. *Just stop,* I tell myself.

Stop moving so I can regain a sense of where I should be.

Thankfully, Lisa sees that I'm struggling and sits down at the dinner table.

I state the obvious. "I'm having a hard time seeing today."

"I could tell when I came into the kitchen."

"Everything blurs into everything," I continue, trying to explain an experience that is impossible to explain.

"Why don't you sit down here and I can make you breakfast?" Lisa's voice is sweet and loving.

My anger flares. "No thanks. I can make my own breakfast."

I turn to find the coffee grinder and smack into the small stainless steel table.

"Fuck. I can't do anything right."

As I start to grope for the counter top, I feel Lisa's hand on my shoulder.

"Marn, just for today, let me make you eggs and toast," she says gently.

I carefully move out of the kitchen and sit down at the table. I listen to her. After five years of this kitchen dance I have finally realized that it is best to sit on these days of change, to let my cells adjust.

As she makes breakfast, I remind myself of the feeling of fall light. It is softer, less piercing than the laser light of summer. In the summer my eyes seek shelter from the light. Once a day I find a dark room and hide in the darkness. Now, as I sit in the deep tones of fall, I begin to sense the inner life of my eyes.

They feel tired. I blink and draw in a deep breath. The fall light, with its muted tones, can bring comfort. If I can just abstain from working so hard to see, I can bathe in this softer light.

Before I accepted these realities, our kitchen dance was more like a rock concert. Doors would slam. Tears would flow. I felt so useless. I felt that the entire art project, creating a farm, was being taken away from me bit by bit.

Brewing underneath the anger was a heavy fear. *Lisa will leave me.* I was convinced that she would eventually see the light of day. *Who in their right mind would want to spend the rest of their lives with a blind person? I'm half the person she fell in love with. This is a burden no one would want to take on.*

Fight. Push back. Push away the pain. Push away the vulnerability of love. I fought every week. She fought back. She was confused. She wanted to love me. Finally, exhausted from fighting, I realized that perhaps she truly didn't mind that I was blind. That we were mates for better or for worse.

Lisa, holding up toilet paper rolls, once said, "I forget about your eye condition because you're such a capable person. I'm sorry, Marn, that I keep forgetting to put things away in the house."

I feel bad about my constant need for order, but the best way for me to move through the world is by memorizing what's around me. Our house is the most restful place for me. I know where the bookcase is, where the stove is, where my bed is. Any time something moves, whether it's furniture, people, lighting, food, or any object, I have to focus and memorize it. It can be exhausting.

That day she held the empty toilet paper rolls up to her eye and looked out at the world around her. She moved her head from side to side for several minutes. Afterward she sat down on the chair. I could tell that she finally understood how little I was able to see. It had been explained to her many times before, but it was only when she herself experienced the narrowing of perception that she was able to understand my fear and frustration.

That day we could see eye to eye. That day we reached an understanding.

*   *   *

As fall moves into winter, long shadows and stormy, cloudy days make it harder for me to experience the farm. I feel my body and world contract. Darkness is all around me. I start having strange experiences.

One night, I suddenly sit up in bed, my heart racing. In the deep darkness of the bedroom, my panic rises. *The world is dark. All I can see is darkness. I cannot see. This is what blindness is like.*

I sit motionless and channel all of my energy into the paranoia.

Am I blind now? Quick! Find some light, any light. I must be blind. I can't experience anything. It's dark. It's quiet. It's all over.

I glance around the room. I can't see anything, not even my own body. The room feels dense and small. I can't perceive any separation between myself and the bed. Finally I turn to my right side to face my open closet. I can make out the dim outline of the clothes hanging. My eyes perceive the heaviness of a wool jacket. I stare at it. I let the weight fill me, bring my body back to the mattress.

I can see the wall now, and the dresser, the chair, the dog on the floor. I feel my heart begin to slow down. *Is Lisa still with me?*

I slowly turn my head, afraid that I might discover that I'm in a dream. I see Lisa's gentle breath move the sheets up and down.

I am alive and I can see. I am in the present and Lisa is here with me. I am not alone.

I slowly ease back into the sheets and turn toward my partner. I hold her hand and marvel at the beauty of her hair.

The sun awakens us with its optimistic light, but my head is still heavy from the fear. I put on my soft, worn farm clothes and head out the door. As I walk down to open the cow gate, I stop and capture a thought. It stuns me. I know why the episode last night was so familiar. This was how my mother must have felt. She couldn't escape her fate, the knowledge of her approaching death. I cannot escape my fate, either. My ability to see will die.

I can't let the fear of darkness destroy my life!

I look at the cows waiting patiently and slowly open the gate. I try to focus my attention on these amazing animals, but the cloud of fear that has been trailing me now settles on me like a thick blanket.

An hour later I'm lying on the bed crying, my head cradled in my hands.

"Marn, are you OK?" Lisa whispers.

"No."

I continue to cry and curl my body into a fetal position. I know that I'm in a state, but I don't know how to get out. The crying turns into sobbing, my entire body condensing into a wet mass. Extreme thoughts run through my mind. *I'm ready to give up. I can't do this any longer.*

The entire winter and spring become colored by periodic breakdowns. A week would run smoothly, and then an incident would trigger a collapse.

One week it was shopping at the health food store. I needed just a few things, but I wanted to linger for awhile, enjoying the colorful fruit and vegetable displays. As I headed toward a bin of gorgeous red apples, I felt a sharp object dig into my thigh. Startled I looked down to see a dozen heads of broccoli scattered on the floor from the produce manager's cart. Blushing, I helped the manager pick up the produce.

I quickly left the produce area. *I don't need vegetables, anyway.*

The store aisles were bustling with mothers and children filling their carts. I stopped briefly to chat with a friend. The small talk soothed my nerves. I gave her a hug to close the conversation and walked down the chips and salsa aisle. Suddenly a child was crying on the floor in front of me. I had knocked her over. Her mother gave me a look that said *"you crazy jerk!"*

I was horrified. I reached out to the child, but she was afraid of me. I tried to talk to the mother, but she turned her back and whisked the little girl away. I stood in silence, staring at the floor. Then I walked to the front of the store, dropped my basket, and walked out.

I'm too dangerous to be shopping alone.

Another incident happened just a few days later. Lisa and I had spent three hours crawling on our hands and knees weeding the cowpeas and sesame seeds. With our bellies grumbling, we were ready to play hooky. A drive into town for a slice of cheese pizza and a cold pilsner sounded like heaven.

We dragged our tired bodies back to the house to get ready. We used the nail brush to scrub away the dirt under our fingernails, threw on our "town" Levis, and brushed our hair.

I sank into the driver's seat, cranked up Annie Defranco, and cranked down the windows. As we drove to town, we laughed with joy. We felt free—free to make our art and free to be our own bosses.

Downtown Grass Valley is a bustling place, but instead of gold miners, it's now filled with weekend tourists. The old Del Oro movie theater still draws large crowds. It's on the main street sharing a four-way stop with the bank, a bar, and a pastie shop.

I pulled the car up to the stop sign and paused, noticing all the people sauntering around our historic town. It was my turn to go.

"Hey! Stop!" Lisa yelled, throwing up her hands. "There are people crossing on the right!"

I turned my head to see a family of four staring at us with terror. I tried to send a look of apology and compassion, but they were too scared to make eye contact. With Lisa's guidance I edged out into the intersection and pulled alongside the movie theater. I sat in stunned silence. Then I cried. I had almost killed someone.

I handed the keys to Lisa and never drove in Grass Valley again.

Bit by bit, month by month, year by year, normal activities had to be eliminated from my life. No more simple desires, like a solitary drive in the country. Skiing, biking, running, and team sports were too dangerous for me and anyone in my path. Even reading was becoming a painful act. After an hour my eyes felt like they could burst from exhaustion. I was becoming the physical manifestation of my visual experience. My entire world was a narrow slit.

I tried to be a good sport. Most mornings I would get up with a renewed dedication to rise above my fears and physical limitations. But despite my good intentions and Lisa's love and care, I felt desperately alone. Alone in darkness.

This visceral fear also bred another terror. Sitting with my mother while she was dying, I had witnessed how fear could slowly eat you to your core. Now I was finding myself in a similar place. Just three years before I'd been riding high in my farmer's bliss, only to have my dreams dashed to the ground.

I feared that the terror would take my mind. I lay awake at night frozen in the thought of losing control over my cognition. I was my mother's daughter. Did that mean that nature would have me follow the same course? Could nature be so cruel?

I desperately needed to find a different way of perceiving myself.

CHAPTER 36

"Go sit in that dark room," Meir instructs me. "I have the heater on so it'll be nice and warm. I want you to sit there for 45 minutes, palming your eyes."

This is my first private session with him. The warmth sounds good—it might burn the San Francisco fog out of my bones. The dark room doesn't. With total blackness in my future, why would I want to sit in a totally dark room now? But I trust this man.

Meir came into my life just in time. The night panics continued to haunt me. My self-confidence was eroding. I felt broken and unable to control my emotional state. Then my dear sister-in-law Gigia gave me his name. She had a friend who was legally blind and had worked with Meir Schneider for years.

"She told me that he's a bit unconventional, but he's the best person to help you," Gigia explained. "He has a school in San Francisco. He teaches classes, workshops, and does one-on-one sessions. I think you should call him."

"What kind of vision problems does he work with?" I asked, thinking that he wouldn't be interested in someone with an incurable disease like mine.

"He works with anyone. My friend has a congenital eye disorder, and she says he has helped her from going totally blind. He works with anyone who has a degenerative disease. Usually he can stop its progression, reverse its course, or dramatically slow down the progression."

I called his office without hesitation. Luckily they had an opening for the next week.

*   *   *

The school is located two blocks from the Pacific Ocean in San Francisco. The day is cold and windy. I can barely make out the red sign above the door. I open it and find myself in a small house that has been converted to a center. In front of me is a staircase. I see a woman groping her way down the stairs. From her wandering eyes I can tell that she is blind.

"Hello. I'm looking for Meir Schneider. Is this the right place?"

"It sure is, honey," she says. I can see now that she's a beautiful, middle-aged woman. Her face is beaming.

"He's right upstairs in the massage room. He's finishing up with a client. Go into the office to the left, and they'll take of you."

They have me sit and wait in the hallway in an odd, oversized chair with checkered fabric. Soon a large, boisterous man bursts out of the room. His eyes slowly take me in. He gives me a lovely, warm smile.

I stare at him in disbelief. I know this person. He's the wonderful man who shops for his family at Other Avenues. I rang him up at the register many times. I look into his eyes and return the warmth. I know that I'll be safe with him.

I spend an hour talking with this solid bear of a man. He relaxes me with his kindness. His confidence gives me hope.

"Whatever the ophthalmologist said to you, don't let that discourage you. Do *not* let his words define who you are. Your body, and in this case your retina, can heal."

Meir Schneider gives me a synopsis of his own history. He was born blind. He had glaucoma, an irregularly curved cornea, opaque lenses, and involuntary eye movements. It was impossible for him to process the light that was entering his eyes.

As a young man, he would ride his bicycle through the streets of Tel Aviv, often returning home with scrapes and bruises. At school he was instructed to read by Braille. Always pushing himself, he became the fastest Braille reader in Tel Aviv. But after school he refused to see himself as a blind person. He would spend countless hours practicing the art of seeing. The act that so many of us perform unconsciously, he was training his brain to learn. It took him 17 years of diligent effort to find new ways to perceive light.

By the time I met him, Meir had helped thousands of patients with dramatic results. His patients suffered from a variety of conditions, including cerebral palsy, MS, strokes, and eye disorders. I knew that my condition was deemed incurable, so I was ready to try anything. I signed up for a winter class so that I would miss fewer farm chores.

I walk into the cozy, warm, very dark room. I grab a chair and pull it close to the massage table. I'm going to palm my eyes using the technique that Meir taught me the day before. I start by rubbing my hands together to create warmth and radiant energy. I place my elbows on the table, take a deep breath, and gently cup my palms over my closed eyes. I am surrounded by darkness. I feel like I'm in a cave. Not a single photon is running around the room. I feel weightless, but I can sense the weighty presence of Meir and his assistants.

Forty people from all walks of life are sitting with me in this dark room holding their palms to their eyes. Like me, they're taking long, deep breaths. Every one of us has a vision problem. In front of me is a young man who has my same eye disease, but already, at age 25, he can only see shadows. To my right is a man from Japan who was a professional baseball player. A ball hit his eye and detached his optic nerve. Sitting in the front row is a woman who has worn thick glasses from the age of two.

The quiet, meditative pose reminds me of my months of Taoist meditation. It allows me to find comfort in the room's stillness. Now if I can just find stillness in my mind for a moment or two.

But instead my mind is racing. I have an urge to turn on the lights so that I can reassure myself that I can still see. Yet the palms of my hands feel so wonderful. I can feel their warmth caress the inside of my eyelids and travel into my eyeballs. I feel the muscles relax. I had no idea that my eyes were so tired, that they were yearning for this type of massage. I take another long, deep breath.

As I exhale, a disturbing flash of light appears in the right corner of my left eye. Then another flash of light appears in my right eye near the periphery. I stop breathing. I think that someone must be opening the door. I take my hands away, but I can see nothing. It's so dark in the room that I cannot even see my hands in front of me.

Where is that light coming from?

I gently place my hands back on my eyes and again feel a wave of relaxation. *This feels good.* Then comes another distraction. I wonder if the 45 minutes are almost up and impulsively turn on the LED light on my watch. *Wow! It has only been 5 minutes!* I try to readjust my attitude and give in to the heat and soothing feeling on my eyelids.

A flash of fireworks burst into view. Now I know that the light is coming from within me, from some previous neural firing. Like the lactic acid in my muscles that makes them sore, this light is tired neurons firing away. Once I make this connection, I'm determined to wait out the light storm and see if I can achieve total darkness. I cannot.

More flashes. The energy is all bound up in there. With the next flash comes a wave of grief. I see hospital beds, the madness in my mother's eyes. I see broken dreams and broken lives.

"Ok, class, slowly open your eyes," instructs the assistant, and I pull myself out of my anguish.

After the palming exercise, we listen to Meir Schneider lecture about the physiology of the eye. He ends with an announcement. "Meet back here at 7 tonight and we'll do our night walk."

A walk in Golden Gate Park at night with 40 other sight-impaired people? I envision people falling into ditches, getting run over by cars, and breaking bones. But everyone else in the room seems to be bubbling with excitement.

We park the car near Mountain Lake. I take a leap of faith as I step out onto the curb. I can hear the busy, urban world a couple of blocks behind me. Here in the park, away from cars, it is still and black. I ask another student for help. I feel Sarah grab my hand.

"Don't worry, Marney. Kelly and I will take care of you," she says. Sarah, who is legally blind with macular degeneration, has the confidence of Julia Childs. I trust her because I know that she has fantastic night-time vision. She can't see the world beyond her outstretched arms, but she can perceive the photons in the night light. This walk will be a total treat for her, especially because she'll have the rare pleasure of helping someone else see.

Walking that night, I quickly realize that I have to give up all notion of being a strong, independent woman. At any moment I can walk into a ditch or fall into the lake. Feeling Sarah's hand on my elbow, I relax and let myself be guided by the humanity between us.

This experience of vulnerability becomes a turning point for me. I begin to find the courage to proceed with my life despite the fear that claws at me every night. I'm learning that there is nothing to fear but the debilitating inaction that fear can cause. I'm learning how to walk right into the fear, to walk right into the dark of the night.

I will soon prove to myself just how far I've come.

CHAPTER 37

I place the last ear of corn in the wheelbarrow. The entire half acre is now harvested. In two weeks we'll plow in the field, and the land will rest until spring.

The season was wonderfully fruitful. We had abundance. The mill house will soon be filled to the ceiling with bins full of beans, pumpkin seeds, sesame seeds, poppy seeds, corn, flax seeds, amaranth seeds, sorghum seeds, and quinoa.

I slowly push the black, rusty wheelbarrow back to the barn, breathing in the sweet, wet grass hay around the compost yard. My body is tired from five months of hard labor, but my mind is energized. With the crops all tucked away, I can now go back to San Francisco and continue to unravel the web of darkness creeping into my eyes.

At the train station I give Lisa a long hug goodbye. I sleepily watch the hills roll by as I imagine the possibilities that await me in the golden city.

*   *   *

I roll my body on the mat so that my left shoulder crushes under my weight. I shift my weight and repeat the motion on the other side. I can feel the enormous weight of my head as my neck tries to keep it from touching the floor.

Meir instructs the class to continue the exercise. After a few minutes I stop worrying that my head will collide with the floor and begin to relax my neck. As the muscles unwind, I suddenly become aware of my body. I stop moving for a second and ponder this incredible awareness. As I slowly begin moving again, tears well up in my eyes. I'm overcome with relief and joy.

I do have a shoulder! The sensation makes me realize how much I've unconsciously detached my mind from my body.

Out of sight, out of mind.

When I was younger, I could see my feet, my hands, my shoulders, even my hair blowing in the wind. Now that I don't see these parts of my body, I've lost my connection to them. I can sense when a person is standing next to me, but I can't determine where my body ends and theirs begins.

We roll for ten full minutes. This exercise is incredibly relaxing. It's helping meet my emotional need to feel whole again. I feel like I'm reconnecting with a dear old friend.

My trusted instructor Meir Schneider insists on constant movement.

"Let's go to the beach," he announces during one of the workshops. Most of the class groans at the thought of the cold Pacific wind on our faces. The room is warm and cozy from our exercises. I smile. I'm ready for the temperature change.

As we make our way to the beach, I choose to walk next to Meir. He holds his body with confidence. It's apparent that he would never lose his balance. The man walks from his belly.

Usually we can see the condition of someone's heart by looking into their eyes. With Meir, since his eyes were damaged at birth, his heart shines through his hands and around his entire face. Both are warm and large.

He stops in front of a beautiful display of wild-flowers and bends over to look more closely. The students gather around him.

"Look at the petals on these flowers. Do you see them?" he shouts over the roar of the ocean.

"Yes, they're beautiful," I shout back, bringing a big smile to his face.

Many of the other students have left their glasses behind, trying to see the world unaided. We wait in silence. In a few moments, some of them begin to whisper excitedly.

"I can see them without my glasses!" a young woman exclaims.

We stand here for a long time. Meir is bent over with his face just inches above the flowers. I watch as he becomes lost in this world, exploring the grooves in the petals, the bee on the leaves, the pollen that remains on the stamen. For a moment he has forgotten the class.

Slowly, as if emerging from a dream, he rises and gives me a pat on the back.

"That was wonderful, eh?"

For Meir, every illuminated object is a treasure. He wants to share his sense of joy and wonderment with us because he believes it's the first step toward healing.

We follow him to the beach, our excitement rising. We wait for our turn at the traffic light, and then all thirty of us practically float across the busy highway. When we reach the overlook, Meir has us pause before descending into the inviting sand.

"Everyone, look to the distance. Look out at the waves coming in. Relax and breathe. We'll stand here for ten minutes."

Once the ocean breeze has relaxed our minds and eyes, we stumble out to the sand. The chattering increases as the whirling sea mist takes away our shyness. The woman standing next to me starts to tell me her life story. I'm astonished to hear her voice. Inside the classroom she huddles mutely against the wall. Now she seems open and ready for life.

The sand is cold on our feet, but the sun is a welcome ball of heat. We're instructed to face the morning sun with our eyes closed. The morning chatter is hushed, and every student melts into a quiet meditation.

"Now gently move your head from side to side. Make sure that you're relaxing your face. Let the warmth of the sun penetrate through," Meir says in a soft, assured voice.

I begin to turn my head from side to side. Immediately I tense up, fearing the sun's intensity will damage my eyes.

Trust the instructor, I tell myself.

A cool wind kicks up off the cold water and engulfs us. I sense the woman next to me pull up the hood of her sweatshirt. The gust subsides, and the sun greets us with a brilliant warmth.

Sun, oh sun, where have you been all my life? I chant to myself, realizing how much I've neglected this supreme orb. I relax into it, letting the sun's photons caress my eyes.

One of my classmates shouts, "What is the purpose of this exercise?"

"By turning our heads from side to side, in and out of the sun's light, we're opening and closing the pupillary muscles and increasing circulation," Meir explains.

I begin to appreciate that these organs of perception actually need the light of the sun for nourishment. My eyes are digesting the light. Like the rest of my body, they need to be reawakened to their role. Just as I rolled from side to side to feel my shoulders, I need to move my head side to side to remind my pupils how to contract and expand in the presence of light.

A leaf needs the sun. The packets of energy in the form of waves touch the surface of the leaf and relinquish their identity. At this point the wave willingly allows the chloroplast of the plant to convert this energy into a chemical useful for the plant.

My eyes need the sun, too. Like the leaf, they take an energetic wave and fold the energy into a molecule. My eyes yearn for the sun. I too need to feed from the natural world. I am part of nature.

When the class is over for the day, I decide to return to the beach. I sit at the edge of the sand so the cold water doesn't drench my feet and watch the waves as they effortlessly ebb and flow. I think about how the sea maintains a constant in and out flow while also moving the water up and down the width of the beach. I think about the beauty of the tide coming in and going out.

I gaze out to the horizon.

My universe has just expanded.

It's nearly sunset and I can see the exact place on the horizon where the sun will dip below the sea. The simple symphony of sounds and rhythms relaxes every nerve in my body.

In and out. Up and down. Day in and day out.

In the case of retinitis pigmentosa, the "tide" doesn't go in and out. Instead, the blood seems to stagnate and pool. The rod cells don't withdraw the fluid from the retina after they've been bleached by the sun. Instead the fluid hangs around, burning permanent images into my eyes.

My mind wanders back to the days I sunned on the beach in San Diego. I remember the countless hours I spent lying on my beach mat and memorizing the movements of molecules as if I were memorizing the items in my beach bag. There was no life in these images, just the need to memorize the chain of events. Now I realize that those molecules are fluid, like the cadre of eye students moving down the beach.

There may be stagnation in my eyes, but I am part of a giant symphony of movement. I can choose to dance, or I can choose to cry.

I can feel my frozen attitude about my eye disease begin to melt. I walk, feeling the sand give under my feet, and sing over and over again:

> *Return again*
> *Return again*
> *Return to the land of your soul*
> *Return to what you are*
> *Return to who you are*
> *Return to where you are*
> *Born and reborn again.*

Rabbi David Zeller

The breeze moves gently in and out of my hair as I jump on the trampoline. I have a small piece of paper over my nose, blocking my central vision. This exercise stimulates my remaining peripheral cells. It feels glorious to soar through the air and let go of the need to see. I relax and let my body receive the light that wants to interact with me. Fuzzy shapes move up and down with my motion. As my body relaxes, I find myself in the present moment.

I'm lucky that I have the freedom on the farm to engage in this healing daily routine. It helps set a grounded tone for the day.

Tomorrow is our monthly CSA farm share distribution so Lisa and I are busy milling flour, measuring beans, cleaning seeds, and filling hundreds of sacks. The sacks are made of soft cotton material with fun patterns that was donated by farm members and relatives. Every month the farm members return the bags to be filled again with flour, dried beans, herbal teas, dried fruits, breakfast cereal, pancake mix and sesame seeds.

I carry a five-gallon bucket filled with sesame seeds from last month's harvest. To harvest them, we cut the four-foot tall stalks and placed them on large tarps. The late summer sun works the stalks, turning them from bright green to a light brown. As the pods changed color, they slowly tightened and gained tension until they burst open and released their seeds into the hot air.

As the seeds spill from my measuring cup into the cloth sack, their nutty aroma fills the air. These are sixth generation seeds, descended from the original seed that we grew six summers ago. Their summer goodness will nourish all of our farm members. The seeds tie us together as a community.

My back is tired, so I walk outside to take a break. I rest my back against the Fuji apple tree, sharing her view of the pond shimmering with fish and aquatic insects. I shift my gaze to the great valley of Sacramento far to the west, letting my eyes tear with relief. I transition smoothly into another eye exercise, gazing far off into the distance for twenty minutes. I feel my eye muscles relax. This brings tears to my eyes. I take deep breaths as my entire body begins to feel the serenity of gazing off into the distance.

My mind floats freely, and I begin to ruminate on my life as a farmer.

*   *   *

Of all the farm tasks, the act of composting is the most satisfying. The subtle alchemy that happens within this innocuous mass meets a deep need in my psyche.

The first morning's light is always accompanied by a fresh, steaming pile of cow dung. The sound of the noisy metal gate wakes the mama cow from her night's meditation. She snorts and moves into an elegant "cow pose," her back arched downward and her head and rear arched toward the sky. Then she eliminates the night's digestion. The morning dew and digestive vapors swirl together and drift toward my nose. I find the wonderful, green smell as appealing as the aroma of brewing coffee. Between the light of the morning and the vapors of the manure, this is one of the mysterious pleasures of farm life.

My job is to collect this lovely, round pie and bring it to the compost yard. Here, within the confines of this dusty, bare lot, begins the culture of the land and my deep involvement in it. It is where our human endeavor called agriculture begins. We combine the manure with straw and other dried materials in order to elevate it to a state that will be most useful for the soil.

When I started farming this wondrous land in the Sierra foothills, I felt overwhelmed by the task that lay ahead of me. My role was to study the contours of the land, listen to the whispers of the creek, and begin to design a farm. I knew from my work with native plants in the Presidio that nature has her grand plan, and it's best to listen to the structures laid down by the topography and climate rather than the ideas coming from my own ego.

I remember how apprehensive I was the first day we sank the plow into the virgin soil. I knew that this gesture would change this little valley for quite some time. I was handed a big dose of humility that day.

We had chosen an acre-sized area to be the site of our first row crop garden. As we began to turn the soil over, I felt how strange it was to have the authority to do such a drastic thing. While we were spading the ground, hundreds of field mammals ran for safety. I felt the weight of my responsibility as director of the "farm show." I was also proud. Every decision was up to me, and certainly every failure from this point on was my doing as well.

I deeply felt my place in the natural world that day. As a human I had the capacity to move this earth and shape this valley. At my mercy were all the wondrous creatures that had fixed themselves here like pieces to a puzzle.

What an enormous responsibility.

What an exciting thrill.

After we finished, Lisa and I stood in the dusk looking out on the brown land that had just been green. I placed my foot on a clod of dirt and slowly crumbled it. It resisted at first and then softly gave way.

We stood there in silence for a long time. Listening, smelling, and soaking in the last light of the day.

That day my grandfather's posture finally made sense to me. As he took his solid strides across his Ozark farm, he was like a seasoned teacher walking into a classroom. He had a humble command of his farm that I admired even as a young child.

I think of him often when I'm walking the farm, and I try to emulate his attitude.

He raised beef cattle, but this description doesn't do justice to how he took those animals into his heart. Years later I heard from my Uncle Charles how my grandfather would stay up all night holding the ears of many newborn calves. He did this to keep their ears from freezing in the cold but also, I'm sure, to comfort them. My brother and I would be snuggled up in our warm beds, unaware that my grandfather spent night after night in that cold barn.

This same gentle spirit would get him up before dawn just to heat up the honey buns and blackberry syrup for his grandchildren. We would sit sleepy-eyed watching him prepare our breakfast. Usually he would hum to himself as he stirred the blackberries, a warm spring light cast on his face. My brother would pull open the curtains, and we would look out onto a world filled with adventure, including the creek we would swim in later that day with my grandmother.

The creek was wide and shallow, cold but not freezing. Where we dipped into the creek was a huge salt lick. Without fail, just as we would wade into the creek, the herd would come to lick their salt and cross to the other field. With their heads held high, their large bodies would delicately move into the stream. The three of us would stop our playing to watch our fellow mammals negotiate the currents.

* * *

The apple tree seems to shake me awake from my daydream. As I begin to walk back to the CSA bag packing area, I feel the pulse of our farm and a connection to the many beings around me. I can sense that they want contact with the human heart and mind, that they want to commune with us. What a comfort this has been, and what unexpected help as I look for guidance in this world.

My feet can find the subtle undulations of the earth. I know the path to and from the yurt. It takes a dip here and a wide turn there where the midday summer sun shines on my forehead. I know the soft path that snakes around the oak grove. It is always dark in there, but I can "see" because the hollow in that valley oak always draws me in. I walk closer and closer to its fragrant ethers then steer away just in time to avoid falling into its hole.

My favorite walk is at the end of the day when we bring the cows in for milking. When the cows are in the far pasture, I must walk past the house, past the compost yard, past the first pasture, through a gully, and across a field where I find them immersed in the juice of the summer grasses.

I could do this walk blindfolded, which I practically do. I can see only a small window of light in front of me, but I fully experience what light there is. As it slowly closes in on me, I find that my enjoyment of the sensual world expands. I may not see the compost piles as I stride past the yard, but I can feel the heaviness that they bring to the ground. The compost has an unmistakable self-importance that it breathes out, so different from the calm, pastoral feeling that I get from the pastures. I notice the changing angle of light as the seasons pass. I can detect the brilliant contrasts of a black nose and a golden coat on my Jersey cow.

Of course, as the visual world fades away, I still become crippled by fear from time to time. I become panic stricken that I will close in myself. I fear that the world will become a narrow, dark hallway with only a pinhole of light. But I can also feel my soul being lifted in new directions like a curious explorer. This feeling is familiar, reminding me of myself as the young scientist and the person who so badly wanted to understand life.

Well here life is, in the compost yard. Just not in a form that I expected.

CHAPTER 39

I'm relaxing in the Santa Cruz sun. My brother Billy is by my side sipping a Corona. He's deep in conversation with Zander, his old friend from college. We've come to Zander's house for a visit. My sister in- law sits across from me, her eyes closed and sunbeams falling across her face. Buzzing around me on the lawn are Lisa and my niece and nephew, who have started to play a game in the lush grass.

"So, are you ready for a tour of the house?" Zander asks, his voice warm and welcoming.

I follow him through the back door and into the kitchen. I pause and sense a hint of the sweet Taoist temple that used to be here. I walk toward the back of the house to what used to be a modest altar. Now it's his son's bedroom. The deep, contemplative light that used to fill this room has been replaced with the sunny optimism of youth. I stand still and let the different light expressions swirl around and within me. It feels good. It feels new and old and reassuring.

I turn around and go back through the house to the living room. I pause where the long oak table used to sit. Here we would soak up the wise words of the Tao Te Ching.

Chapter 11

Thirty spokes join at the hub to make a wheel
Yet the usefulness of the wheel is found in the gaps
Mold and fire clay into pots and vessels
And where there is nothing the usefulness of the pot is
found.

Cutting out doors and windows we make a house
But it is the open/emptiness that give the house its
usefulness

Therefore we see that it is in the substance of a thing
we find benefit,
But in the emptiness of a thing we find its use.

translated by Charles Belyea

The words have a deeper meaning to me now.

I walk back out into the glorious Santa Cruz
sun, smiling to myself as I sit down next to my brother.

Billy seems surprised at how calm I appear.
"Don't you think it's bizarre that my good friend lives in
the house where you used to study Taoism? I think it's
an incredible coincidence."

"It doesn't surprise me. It just makes me happy.
I view it as a sign that I'm on track with my life. It reminds me of spending time in the woods with Darwin."

"Darwin? What makes you think of him?"

I laugh. "You may think that he was just a dog,
but he was my first teacher in Taoism. We'd take these
long walks together. I usually took that book of ancient
poetry that Tom, remember my high school friend, gave
me. After a snack, I'd sit and read, and, while I'm trying
to make sense of these abstract poems, Darwin would

be sniffing around weaving an elaborate web of 'now-ness.' It was an early lesson in how to be in the present moment."

My dear brother turns his generous smile on me. We know that we don't need any more words. We just sit and enjoy each other in silence. I begin to lose myself in memories of the years I spent cultivating the Tao. In my mind I see a gold thread, a stunning light that brings a small tear of joy to my eye.

Later in the day we hug Zander, my brother, and his family goodbye, and Lisa and I head back to the farm. We stop at Emily's Bakery for a poppy seed muffin and a hearty cup of coffee to fortify us for the five-hour drive. We wind around the coastal range and in and out of the majestic redwoods. Finally we leave the great valley behind and ascend into the Sierra foothills.

Each year on the farm, I plant many seeds. I tend to their need for food, water, and sunshine. I apply generous amounts of compost to the garden bed, making a rich, humus womb for the seeds to lie in. Then I let the soil have a long drink of water. This will usually wake the seeds from their long slumber.

Of course, it also wakes up the many weeds that will try to crowd out my little newborns. So I tend to another important need: removing competition for the sunlight and other resources. This tending lasts the entire spring and well into the summer months. During these months I wake up in the morning thinking, *What plant needs my attention today?*

For most plants, the month of July is a turning point, and they reach a type of homeostasis. They seem to have found their niche and are busy producing flowers. Each plant reaches for the heavens with its version of sexual organs. No wonder the bees and other insects are humming with such excitement!

The plants' final act is so subtle, so lacking in fanfare, that I always seem to miss it. I'll be busy running around the farm watering when, all of a sudden, I'll stop dead in my tracks.

Oh my, look at that seed pod! When did that happen? I say to myself in dismay. I bend down and gently take the pod in my hand. Unlike the rest of the plant, the pod seems to have a tight, compact energy. It's so different from the bloom with its delicate, airy, whimsical expression. The plant is returning from its wonderful end point of expansion back to where it started, condensed into a seed.

I look around the farm. The corn is expressing the same rhythm. The tassel is this lovely, wispy finale of such a beautifully designed, compact seed package. And, yes, the sorghum is doing the same expression of contraction. And look at the cowpeas!

It's like an orchestra, with all of the plants playing a crescendo as they reach the height of their expansion, followed by the decrescendo of contraction. It's easy to think of each plant having an individual nature. But if instead I tune my perceptions to see that the plants are expanding and contracting in response to something bigger than themselves, I can perceive the grand expansion of summer, followed by the condensing of fall, and the final movement inward at winter. These continuous, subtle movements of energy are so profoundly simple that we tend to ignore them.

If plants are connected to this dance, then I must be, too. And so must the cows, and even the dragonflies. I begin to see this expression of energy all around me, to see that we are all dancing to this heavenly vibration.

So when I plant the seed in the fertile womb every spring, she moves from this tight seed to a seedling, to a mature plant, to a seed again. What poetry!

When I held my mother's hand as she was dying, I felt the lightness of her being. She hovered over the room as if she were pollen being released from the corn tassel. I didn't understand it at the time. But now I can see that it was a beautiful, graceful gesture, to move from her body's compaction to a light, airy, amorphous being.

This thought brings me great comfort.

CHAPTER 40

The rooster crows and stirs the warm air around my head. My consciousness shifts, and I can sense that my sheepdog Sidney is awake and watching the dawn from our bedroom porch. The heat makes it easy to open my eyes.

I gaze at Sidney and trace the outline of her graceful, athletic body. Her muscles are relaxed but ready to spring into action. Next to me I can hear Lisa's steady breathing. The sound is comforting and soothing. The sound, rhythm, and smell of her breath make me feel at home.

The dog barks. Lisa stirs and reaches out to me. I turn toward her and we hold hands. My eyes drift to the painting on the wall at the end of the bed. I never tire of looking at it. It's a wonderful symphony of colors playing off each other in abstract freedom. The paints are treated so that the colors are nearly transparent. Blues blend into blacks and finally into reds. When I look at the abstract shapes, I feel like I can almost see behind the colors.

My eyes focus on the narrow, red rectangle that seems to peek out of the composition. It's off center, near the bottom half of the painting.

Nice job, Mom. I smile to myself. It so perfectly rounds out the painting. My eyes move to the BBlair in the bottom right corner. As a child in Boulder I watched her practice this signature countless times. I remember how she devoted hours, years, and decades to the study of light and color. Her devotion beams through this sweet painting on my wall. The colors, *her* colors, travel into my eyes.

I'm jolted from my meditation by the sound of Sidney dashing out into the yard. Soon I hear her out near the periphery of the farm, barking at some predator making its way back to its den. The ruckus gets Lisa out of bed, and she heads to the kitchen. Java is on the way.

I turn back to the painting. Now that I'm alone in the warm bed, I let my body relax. I feel the painting's quality of light and combination of colors relax the muscles around my eyes. It feels soothing and nourishing.

I let myself move deeply into this visual relaxation. Without effort, my mind begins to create whisperings of images. I travel deeper and begin to feel enveloped in memories of Beverly. These memories have a different quality than those stored in my cortex. It is as if they're moving on an internal wind, freely associating. My eyes, now fully relaxed, travel beyond the colors to an energy within the colors and land on the soft, delicate color of Beverly's hair.

The gurgle of the espresso pot snaps my mind back to the present and the day's farm chores. The sun isn't up over the horizon yet, but the farm animals' appetites are awakened by the pre-dawn crow of the roosters.

It amuses me to watch the urgency of the chickens as they're released from their coop. I can hear the ruckus inside the coop as I approach with the buckets full of food. A hen squawks as I unlatch the door, and then, like shopper's at a Macy's white sale, all of the chickens come rushing out. I quickly stand aside to let them have the room they need. Some start drinking water, while others gather around the feeder like New Yorkers at a luncheon counter. Others run to the rock outcrop to scratch for bugs.

The pigs run quickly to me as I approach, their snouts wiggling as they smell their breakfast. They, of course, have similar enthusiasm for their morning gruel. But unlike the high-pitched squawks of the hens, they snort with joy. Their snorting is so rapid fire that it sounds like a snort-laugh. Like the chickens, they dive into the food enthusiastically as soon as it slops into the trough. Their flat pink snouts wrestle for their shares, afraid that there may not be enough.

This eating frenzy is precisely why it's so important to have a good, strong cup of coffee beforehand. The caffeine stirs my blood enough to keep me on my toes. Several times I've had to discourage the frantic pigs from eating my pant leg, which they've mistaken for whey-soaked corn.

I walk toward the gate that the cows pass through to get their food. Lisa and a third grade class built it. It is decorated with twenty-four, stamped metal rectangles that the students made by hammering nails into sheet metal to create patterns. Some of the patterns are stars, others trees and houses, and a few are abstract. The rectangles hang randomly on the gate, creating a playful display.

As I open the gate, the cows move through and up the chute to the corral, where flakes of alfalfa and grass hay are on the ground waiting for them. Unlike the chickens and pigs, they walk in a state of sleepy meditation. Their massive bodies move with surprising grace. They bob their heads at me as they pass. Each takes a bit of the flake and tosses it in the air to break it apart. Soon they settle in and slowly chew their meal.

My friend Maya walks down the driveway.

"You're gonna show me how to make butter this morning, right?" she asks, with child-like excitement. I place my arm affectionately over her shoulder, and we walk into the milk processing room. On the table is a five-gallon container filled with very cold milk from last night's milking.

The thick, viscous cream has defied gravity and risen to the top, and the thinner milk has separated to the bottom. I grab a stainless steel ladle from a hook on the wall and use it to gently swirl the rich, top layer. Slowly the cream flows into the ladle, and I pour it into a mason jar. When the jar is filled to the brim with thick white cream, I pour one third of the volume into another glass jar, seal it tightly, and begin to shake vigorously. I shake for five minutes, listening to the glub, glub of the liquid hitting the sides of the jar.

When I can no longer hear the sound, I know that the cream is too thick to be agitated, but I continue to shake it anyway. Suddenly it feels different. I look at the jar and it appears as if I've shaken a yellow mass free of the white cream. I shake it again, and the yellow form is easier to make out. I shake one final time, and the solid, yellow mass has precipitated out and is swimming in a thin, white liquid.

"How does it do that, Marn?" Maya asks, astounded by the process even though she's the one with a masters in chemistry. "Where does the vibrant yellow come from? The cream was white."

I just look at her and grin. "It's magical, don't ya think?"

I salt the butter and divide it into half-pound packages. They'll stay in the freezer until winter, when we'll use them for pies and breads.

Once I've tended to the animals and the milk, I can focus on myself and my eyes for awhile. Out of both pleasure and necessity I spend time doing my eye exercises daily. Without them I'm crippled by migraines. Not long ago, I resisted the daily routine of stimulating my periphery, walking backwards, flashing lights, and palming. Now I welcome the routine. I embrace the release that happens within my nervous system, and I embrace the beauty that is light. Beauty that Beverly spent most of her life pursuing, and a beauty that I now enjoy.

I close the office door behind me to muffle the summer chatter and find enough quiet to unravel the fatigue within my eyes. The room is very dark, and I can smell the sweetness of frankincense. It offers the perfect escape from the intense, summer sun.

I turn the timer to 35 minutes. I sit at a table and place my palms over my closed eyes. I love this posture. I can feel my body begin to let go. At first I see flashes of light, as my retinal cells continue to react as if there's light to perceive. Within a couple of minutes, however, I can see total darkness, an achievement that comes with many years of practice. I can perceive a darkness that is as black as the tip of my dog's nose. It isn't scary anymore. In fact, I find it as relaxing as a swim in a cool pool.

The longer I sit with my warm palms soothing my eyes, the more relaxed my eyes become. Sometimes when they're in this state, I begin to have spontaneous light memories that are very vivid and feel like a part of me. Occasionally, in my eye's imagination, the light extends around to the side of my head. At this moment I can feel the expansion of what I used to perceive. My body stretches there to find the vestiges of a larger, more expansive me.

I too can expand beyond myself.